THE SECRETS ING,

AUTHENT I

COLORS OF THE MIND

Fraya Mortensen

Colors of The Mind

The author of this book does not dispense medical advice or prescribe the use of any technique as a form of treatment for physical, emotional, or medical problems without the advice of a physician. The intent of the author is only to offer information of a general nature to help you in your quest for emotional well-being. In the event you use any of the information in this book for yourself, the author assumes no responsibility for your actions.

All names used throughout the book have been changed to protect identity and privacy

Published 2023

Cover and Interior Design by Verity Casey

ISBN: 978-1-7380442-0-7

Acknowledgements

Thank you to my previous employer of 20 years, the Ministry of Community Safety and Correctional Services, Ontario Canada, who gave me the opportunity and training to learn the key concept presented in this book "Colours." Also thank you to my former assistant Christina Hackett who came up with the name of this book.

Contents

Preface 9

Introduction 13

1. Mindset Foundations 17

What is an Attitude? 18
Faulty Foundations in Programming 21
Automatic Thoughts 23
Preparing To Reprogram 25

2. The Four Mindsets: The Mindset Tool Of All Mindset Tools 31

Changing Our Thoughts to Change Our Behavior 32
Our Thoughts Are Manifesting Our Reality 32
The Green Attitude 35
The Red Attitude 37
The Blue Attitude 39
The Purple Attitude 40
It's Very Green To Notice When You're Not Being Green. 42
Bringing the Colors Together 42

3. How Are You Being? 45

An Attitude Is Not A Behavior 47
Lending Money From a Green Attitude 47
The Red Attitude Lends Money 49
The Blue Attitude Lending Money 50
The Purple Attitude Lending Money? 51
The Four Trauma Responses 52
The Four Trauma Behaviors: Fight, Flight, Fawn, & Freeze 54

4. How To Take 100% Responsibility For Your Life 57

What Am I Responsible For? 59
What is an Inside Cue? 59
What is an Outside Cue 60
Reframing your 'Triggers' 61
Practice makes progress, not perfect! 64
Which Mindset Blames Others? 65
Which Mindset Blames Themselves ? 66
Which Mindset Operates From The Highest Form Of Personal Responsibility? 67
The Difference Between Independence and Hyper Independence 69
Independence Vs. Interdependence 70

5. How Validation and Invalidation Influences our Behavior 71

Internal and External Validation 72
How To Change Unwanted Behaviors 73
The Red Thief 73
The Blue Thief 74
People-Pleasing 76

6. Insecure Attitudes in Relationships 79

Dave & Suzy 80
When the Mask Comes Off 84
The Shift Out of Blue Thinking 85
Introverts & Extroverts 88
Rohan and Anna 90
The Insecure Red, Blue and Purple Relationships 94

7. The Secure Green Attitude 97

Erik and Lewis 98
The Green Attitude Does No Harm 100
The Relationship Teeter-Totter 102

8. Feeling Your Feelings 105

What Would Each Of The Colors Think About Their Feelings? 108
Anger 108

Happiness 110
Sadness 112
Empathy 113
Feelings are Information 114
Saying Sorry For Feelings 117
Being Responsible For Your Feelings and Holding Space For Others 118

9. Setting Boundaries 121

How Do I Set Boundaries With Myself? 123
Get In The Driver's Seat of Your Life 125
Balance is Found In Boundaries 126
Emotional Boundaries 127
Which Color Attitude Struggles With Emotional Boundaries? 129
Mental Boundaries 130
Boundaries From a Different Perspective 132
Boundaries Build Bridges Not Walls 133
The Mindset Where Boundaries are Made 139
Internal Boundaries and External Boundaries 141
From Boundaries to Being 142

10. The MindfulGreen Attitude 145

Mindfulness is Everything 146
Finding The Middle Path: Mindful Being vs. Mindless Doing 147
Getting Out of Our Heads & Into Our Bodies 151
Developing Your Mindfulness Muscle 152

11. Purpose, Potential and Intuition 155

Knowing Your Potential 156
Knowing Your Purpose 159
Trusting Your Intuition 163

Summary and Excersises 167

Notes and References 173

Preface

Most people know me as "empathic coach" on the popular social media sites Instagram and Tiktok. I made a video last year where I broke down the elements of a people pleaser and it was seen across these platforms by over 7 million people. I wrote this book because I wanted to share my way of thinking and viewing the world with as many people as possible, aside from a 60 second video. The way I speak is simple, direct and to the point. It's the way I like to be spoken to, and so I try to convey my thoughts and experiences in the same way.

I've always found psychology and human behaviour fascinating and since I also love to write it makes sense for me to write a book about human behavior and how to harness the power of your conscious mind. This book incorporates my 20 years experience working for the Ministry of Correctional Services and Community Corrections in Ontario, Canada as a Probation and Parole Officer. Working within the provincial government gave me access to the best of 'what works' research and training. I was afforded several developmental opportunities during my career which included training other probation officers and facilitating educational and intensive programming to thousands of clients over the years in the area of healthy relationships, substance use, relapse prevention, how to change their thinking, get a job, choose better friends, you name it!

My role within the government also had me completing thousands of in-depth assessments to determine someone's risk level in the community and hundreds of sentencing reports for courts in Ontario outlining comprehensive social backgrounds, and making recommendations as to what would best serve them and the public at large. As a result I became a skilled interviewer who could understand the nuances of each person's family, education, employment, pastimes, addictions, peers and relationship backgrounds that led them to such unconventional behaviors, rendering me an expert in human behavior and mindset.

An American psychiatrist, and best selling trauma research author, Dr. Bessel van der Kolk says that 100 percent of the inmates in the correctional system are actually traumatized children. These were the people I worked closely with to assist them in changing their belief systems and coping skills. With trauma comes thoughts such as "I'm worthless" or "Bad things happen, because I'm a bad person", "Good things happen if I'm a good person" and "If I'm hurt, I must deserve it".

It wasn't until the last four years of my career, while I was managing approximately twenty of the highest risk offenders, that I started to implement a new strategy with them in our meetings together. For these individuals, it wasn't a matter of *if* they'd go back to jail again, but when. Because I was already one of the few people trained in my office to facilitate intensive group programs for clients struggling with substance use, healthy relationships, and relapse prevention, as well as training other probation officers across the province how to run these groups in their offices and within the correctional institutions, I was afforded an opportunity to study a new program that would come with three years of mentorship. I was learning to coach people using a cognitive restructuring tool that was used in Sweden and Canadian Correctional systems called STICS (Strategic Training Initiative in Community Supervision)[1]

I started implementing these tools in my sessions with clients to help them change their attitudes. The most amazing thing about learning this tool is that while we were learning this method to use on our clients, we were also applying it to ourselves. Sounds strange that a tool that was intended to be used on people who broke the law, could also be so beneficial for those who were delivering the tool. With this new method in place, I was not only witnessing changes to my clients behavior, I was also noticing shifts to my own behaviors as well. For those of us participating in this mentoring program, we reported increased job satisfaction and increased clarity and motivation to overcome whatever might have been holding us back in our own lives.

Instead of role playing with client examples, we would

often discuss issues happening in our own relationships or at work, which immediately led to huge transformational shifts. I immediately fell in love with what I was learning and couldn't wait to have the rest of my office experience this new way of working with our clients.

It is known that many people who enter into helping professions are highly empathic, and experience traits of codependency and people pleasing behaviors. It would be a struggle for some of my colleagues to grasp the concepts of the tool to effectively deliver the lessons unless they were also able to grasp the concept of emotional boundaries and personal responsibility. Like any tool, you have to embody it and know it inside and out for it to be effective.

A lot of money was spent by the Ontario Government to train and mentor those involved in this new initiative and it would cost even more to eventually train the whole province of probation officers. The Union representatives complained that it was teaching probation officers "clinical work" and turning us into social workers instead of authority figures, which many were still attached to as the primary focus of our work. Ultimately the expense of the mentorship could no longer be supported by the Ontario Government but lucky for me, by this time in March 2020, I had already completed my mentorship.

In March 2020 COVID-19 struck and everyone was sent home in a lockdown worldwide. This acted as the catalyst for me to resign from my position as a probation officer, leaving behind my 20 year career as a public servant to become an online coach. I obtained my coaching certification in December 2020 and with these new tools in place, I started to coach people worldwide who wanted to overcome limiting mindsets and influence new behaviors.

My growing social media following remarked how the way I spoke was different from what they were hearing in the mainstream and that they were learning things from my short 60 second videos that they'd never heard spoken of in even ten years of therapy. Some of my clients had never worked with a therapist or a coach before, but felt so aligned with what I was talking about, as if I was speaking directly to them, that they saw this as their sign to enroll in my coaching program.

Colors Of The Mind is the result of everything I've learned in my career, my personal philosophy and my intuitive knowledge of what is needed to bring inner peace and authenticity to each and every one of us. When you embrace all of your thoughts and see them as all beautiful colors, it allows us to become more conscious of the thoughts we are choosing to accept.

Colors of The Mind is a book in which I share my philosophy of life in hopes that it aligns with where you need to take yourself so you too can have a more fulfilling life. The common language that I present in the Colors of The Mind allows us all to be on the same page, regardless of our differences.

I hope you will teach these concepts to your children, your grandchildren, your significant others and be a role model for what you will come to learn in this book as "Green Thinking"

Intr

I think it's sa… ation and freed… know this because m… me tell me they want to … Working in the Canadian Crim… years has exposed me to thousa… ed freedom. Whether they were physi… experiencing the loss of freedom to exist … they were constrained by their own chains of j… shame––they yearned for the ability to do what the… This is because freedom is what every human being is … for.

The intention of this book is to lay out the pragmatics of the inner psychological processes of transformation. Within these pages you will be given an opportunity to explore a new way of thinking and perception about the world we live in. This book will teach you how to be your most authentic self through accepting others in the world, regardless of their values, beliefs, attitudes, or biases.

I'm here to give you tools that can change your state in real time. You will become more of a conscious *being* just by reading this book which will lead to being more of a conscious *thinker*. So, the question is, which one comes first? Beingness or thinking? I will propose to you that beingness is our natural state, which is a state of mindfulness where you can then be a noticer of your thoughts, an observer of your thoughts and not entirely your thoughts because they are simply a byproduct of your being.

- A Gentle Warning & Disclaimer -

Take this book in small doses. Give yourself time after each section to let it all sink in. Some of what you read might offend you. If you are not open to accepting truths about yourself, some of the content may stir up confusion, anger, or defensiveness. If you are open to hearing it, then you may instead experience some anxiety. This anxiety is healthy though; it is alerting you to the things you may need to change. You may have to get very uncomfortable first--before you can shift into a new state of being.

This "shifting" is where transformation takes place. Like the seed planted in the cold, dark earth that can't see the light--it doesn't yet know its purpose. Even as the seed starts to crack open, it's still void of any knowledge of its path--but somehow it still trusts the natural processes of life. Just as the sprout must emerge from the seed, this "cracking" is how you will have been "cracked open" too. This can bring on fear and anxiety for those who are unaware of the change process. The cracking of the seed is of its outer shell, just like yours. It's just an old skin that is going to peel off, so that something beautiful and new can emerge.

Going through the information in this book may also make you feel physically sick. This is due to new energy and awareness stirring up inside of you. This new energy and awareness may not mix with the old beliefs you've been hanging onto, causing them to fight each other. This is called "cognitive dissonance," which means that the way you want to behave isn't lining up with your beliefs. This is also called "ascension" in the spiritual world, which means waking up to a new reality. It takes time for change to assimilate and acclimatize into your new being. Give yourself grace, and be kind and gentle with yourself.

Just remember that in order for true healing to occur, it requires that we go into the pain. If you're ready to make some profound shifts in your life, I promise that it will make so many things so much easier down the road. I am so happy that you are here. Thank you for joining me on this journey towards manifesting fulfilling lives filled with peace and prosperity!

Sincerely,

Fraya

1

Mindset Foundations

"If you can build a muscle, you can build a mindset."

JAY SHETTY

What is an Attitude?

When people talk about their attitude, what do you think this refers to? The typical reply I get is "It's how I present myself" or "It's how you are as a person". Sometimes I hear people say "oh like if you have a bad attitude?" as well as "it's a behavior, as in how I present myself," or, "it's the impression people give off to others."

What's important to know is that an attitude is *not a behavior*. Your attitude has much more to do with your thinking and for the purposes of this book, an attitude will be defined as "a collection of thoughts." Our entire lives consist of collecting thoughts. Did you know that humans have up to 70,000 thoughts a day? Wow! Did you also know that the majority of our thoughts are negative, and of those, they are mostly repetitive? That's a not-so-awesome fact about our thoughts. What is awesome about thoughts is that *you can alter them*. All that is required is a dedication to becoming a more conscious thinker.

What is the purpose of being a *conscious* thinker? First of all, through awareness, you can mitigate negative thoughts from consuming your subconscious mind. A powerful tool to help with this is meditation. If you set a timer right now for just one minute with the intention of sitting silently in order to observe your thoughts--you'll find that entire stories are carried on inside your head, without you even being aware of them! There's so much going on that we can't even verbalize --and this was just one single minute! Imagine what goes on over the course of sixteen hours or more while your mind is awake. For those who have difficulty sleeping, I'm sure you can guess what might be keeping you up, those darn thoughts!

We have thoughts about so many things that are not obvious to us, right down to the nuanced flavors of the foods we eat, like the flavor of candy or chips. I love the Zesty Dorito flavor, but not the regular Dorito flavor, because that's my personal preference. Similarly, I like football because of the action and athleticism, but I dislike hockey because of the loud screechy sounds of the arena, as well as there being a higher level of violence in the sport, from what I remember anyway. These thoughts are formed from our responses to external stimuli, and then these thoughts form the beliefs that some chips and sports are better than others. Obviously others have different beliefs from my own (more commonly referred to as opinions); and this is because whatever we *believe* is what is *true* for each of us--and from there, our attitude is formed.

What is much more important than your thoughts about chip flavors or sports are your thoughts about yourself. For however many years you have been living on this earth, you have been forming an attitude *about yourself*. This can be based on so many factors: like how you were raised, what others constantly tell you about yourself, your education, your friendships, your body, your intelligence, etc.

Do any of these thoughts sound familiar to you?

- "I hate my thighs."
- "I've never been satisfied with my appearance."
- "I value my health, and I work hard to take care of it."
- "My hair never does what I want it to do."
- "I'm content with my appearance."
- "I'm terrible at remembering people's names."
- "I love meeting new people."
- "I suck at math."
- "I'm a great problem solver."
- "If it wasn't for bad luck, I'd have no luck at all."
- "I enjoy the mysteries of life."
- "I can't trust myself."
- "I have no idea who I really am."
- "I'm a horrible cook."

Your thoughts about yourself have likely been taking up space in your mind for quite some time, and now they've been programmed to the point where you believe them to be true. Thus, you develop a general attitude, which might not match who you really are on the inside. You might not realize it yet, but *you are in control* of whether or not you accept the thoughts your mind loops through continuously throughout the day. Once you start questioning the validity of your thoughts, you can then start to change them--which will create an entirely new reality for yourself and your life.

In the book, *The Law of Attraction*, by Esther and Jerry Hicks, they write: "The one who speaks most about illness has illness; when you see that the one who speaks most about prosperity has prosperity, you get what you think about, whether you want it or not."[2] Your reality isn't just related to your thoughts about yourself, it's also about the thoughts you have about other people.

Here are some examples of how we think about other people in our lives:

- "My mom is a narcissist."
- "I am so grateful for my sister."
- "My friends are always taking advantage of my kindness."
- "I'm lucky to have some great people in my life."
- "No one understands me"
- "Everyone is a jerk"
- "I appreciate the lessons I've learned from people in my life."
- "Some people are really bad and deserve what they get."

Just as the thoughts you have about yourself become programmed and automatic, so too do your thoughts about other people. They then create a false reality of what you will inevitably experience in your external world--because your opinion about what to expect from others has been imprinted and accepted as truth. When we stay attached to our thoughts, this doesn't leave much room for change, which is a necessary component for compassion and empathy.
Take for example what some people's thoughts are about the homeless:

- "They just need to get a job."
- "They have mental health issues and need help."
- "They're all drug addicts."
- "The government is at fault for letting this happen."

Or consider thoughts that people have about those who are financially successful:

- "They are so lucky to be rich."
- "They must have worked hard to reach financial success."
- "They can't be happy and have all that money."
- "They must have had rich parents and had it all handed to them."
- "It's stressful to have so much money when it can be lost in a second."

Regardless of whether these thoughts are true or not–– they shape our belief systems. Beliefs can change when you become aware and open to new ideas. For example, People used to think that the earth was flat, and it wasn't until science proved that we are orbiting in space with other planets that are the same shape, that they discovered that Earth is not flat at all. Even when evidence to the contrary is presented, our minds have difficulty accepting new information. It can be cumbersome to do so when we've been led to believe something else for so long. When we're given new information it's rare to accept it right away. We need time to process the new info, and at first we may even reject it to preserve the safety of our old reality.

Faulty Foundations in Programming

Psychologists believe that by the age of seven is when our beliefs and our habits are formed. In the first seven years of life, we are highly influenced by others' attitudes as we are exposed to various experiences, influences, and social conditioning. The formation of belief systems is influenced by factors such as family, culture, education, personal experiences, and interactions with others. While beliefs can evolve and change over time, the foundation is typically established during these early stages of life. If you think of yourself like a computer with an internal operating system, those early years are when the hardware and software of your belief system are being installed. Take for example a child's belief in Santa. This belief is well supported by our parents and society based on its basic customs of asking Santa for gifts, etc. As children, we believe that our good behavior will be rewarded with that special toy we've been asking for on Christmas morning. However, when our favorite toy isn't delivered, a new belief forms from either our parents, telling us "the elves ran out of supplies," or "be grateful for what you received." We may create a false belief about ourselves, that we were not good enough or loveable enough to receive our beloved gift in the first place.

One thing that will happen with our beliefs over time, is that they become outdated, and unless we're mindful enough to install our hard drives with necessary updates, we'll forever be operating from an old system. In the example of a child's belief in Santa, over time they receive information that has them questioning the possibility of how someone can fly with reindeer in the sky and fit through people's chimneys with all of those presents. The evidence to disprove this belief becomes obvious and they soon find out that others have foregone this belief as well.

They will have a difficult time letting go of this belief if it has brought them comfort in the past, and they may decide to hold on a bit longer, just to see. To see the next time Santa is supposed to make an appearance and then they may say, "How could I have believed in something so silly." What remains however is the core belief that came years before that telling them that they're not loveable or good enough. The belief about Santa and the belief about oneself are both subject to faulty programming and require the same process in order to make a shift.

Automatic Thoughts

We will always have belief systems in place that are more difficult to challenge and overcome than others. As a result we experience frustration with ourselves and others as we try to shift onto a different path but keep finding ourselves in the same place. It's like what Einstein says about insanity: Insanity is doing the same thing over and over and expecting different results. These habits are our automatic responses to everyday situations, stressors and challenges. You may or may not know it, but the majority of our brain is operating from autopilot. Research in fields like cognitive neuroscience and psychology has shown that a significant portion of our mental processes occur unconsciously.The brain saves energy by relying on unconscious or automatic processes for certain tasks. When a behavior becomes automated or habitual, it requires less conscious effort and cognitive resources to perform. This allows the brain to conserve energy for more demanding cognitive activities.

We have created these well worn pathways over the course of our lives to drive us to work, tie our shoes, make toast, or brush our teeth--all unconscious acts. You no longer have to think about doing these things, you just do them naturally. It's a great way for our brains to conserve energy. But what ends up happening when you have to drive to a new place for a work meeting? Or you get a new pair of shoes that are really hard to get on? Or you have to make toast without a toaster? Or after a recent visit, the dentist tells you that you have gum disease, and that your evening routine now needs to involve flossing, mouthwash, and other practices that you haven't used before.

You may notice the relationships you've been in have had the same unconscious patterns of behaviors too. We may leave an unsatisfying relationship just to enter another one that ends up being exactly the same--even if it appeared to be opposite at the start. We think we'll do it *differently this time*, but because our attitude has stayed the same, so do our outcomes. If you want to go somewhere else, but you keep using the same path to get there, you'll end up exactly where you don't want to be. How does this happen?

I'll tell you how it happens, with the same thinking that got you there in the first place, because *every single behavior is a result of the way we think.*

Our relationships stay the same because our thoughts behind them are keeping it that way. Automatic thoughts will always choose the same pathways because that's what is most familiar and takes the least amount of our energy. Think about going into a new grocery store and not knowing where anything is. It will likely take us twice as long to get all of the items on our list. We prefer familiarity and predictability because it's easier and we don't have to use as much energy to get things done. The new grocery store may have a better selection to choose from, but we'll keep going back to the old one because of its familiarity and convenience.

In the case of those relationships, or the grocery store that we keep going back to, despite their poor quality, our thoughts may be telling us:

- "It's not that bad."
- "Maybe they will change."
- "I'm too tired to try something new"
- "This is normal and just the way it is."
- "All relationships get to this point, so I just have to suck it up."

When we've been conditioned into patterned and predictable behaviors, It's hard work to forge a new path. It takes a lot of energy to clear the tall grasses, get rid of old belief systems and risk getting stuck in the mud, having setbacks, and even getting lost from time to time, and feeling like a failure. This is because many of us are comfortable in the comfort zone, even if it's not that comfortable there. It's predictable. If you say, "No more, I'm done living in these unhealthy patterns," and you attempt to take the road less traveled, not only is this uncomfortable for you, it also may be uncomfortable and look strange to others, because they're stuck in their patterns too. Change will never occur until we've had enough of the discomfort that urges us to steer in a new direction.

By now you're starting to catch on to all of this. Since the majority of our thoughts are stored in our subconscious brain, this tells us that the majority of our thinking is automatic and is prone to making unconscious decisions. The autopilot takes us down those well worn familiar paths, just like the back of our hands and afterwards has us ask ourselves, "What was I thinking?" or say, "I wasn't thinking."

But the truth is:

WE'RE ALWAYS THINKING!

John Kabbat Zinn, head of the center of Mindfulness-Based Stress Reduction (MBSR), says that mindfulness is the ability to be in the present moment, on purpose, without judgment as if your life depended on it. Well, your life does depend on it, because when you go around questioning yourself like, "what was I thinking?" you're not being a conscious person. You are not being responsible. Instead you're being a conditioned robot who is assimilating to a life of conformity. Many individuals are so unaware of their existence they almost cease to exist by default, just by allowing the subconscious mind to run the show. That might sound a bit dramatic, but it's definitely what is happening.

The point? Stop being a programmed robot.

Preparing To Reprogram

After we've done things so many times to the point in which it's become a habit, our body knows the behavior better than the mind. To transition from doing what we no longer want to do and to get better outcomes, we need to become so familiar with our thoughts that prevent us from changing. It's important to note what these thoughts are as they are the ones that form our faulty limited belief system, or what I like to call *stinking thinking*. There are many cognitive distortions that humans have developed such as all or nothing thinking, emotional reasoning, justifying, minimizing, denying, blaming, rationalizing and catastrophizing, to name a few. These errors in our thinking are what we need to fix.

The first step is to take note of the thoughts you've been collecting, and accepting, which have now formed the foundation of your reality. Take a moment to think of ten things that are true including truths about yourself.

1 ____________________

2 ____________________

3 ____________________

4 ____________________

5 ____________________

6 ____________________

7 ____________________

8 ____________________

9 ____________________

10 ____________________

If it took you some time to think of ten beliefs you have or you were not able to come up with even a few, this may be a result of your hardwiring. It takes a lot of energy to become a conscious thinker, as much as negative thinking does. So how would you like to make the most of your energy reserves?

Did you question your abilities? Or did you write about the decent human that you are? Maybe a bit of both? The next step is to take a few moments to answer the questions about your beliefs below:

- Do you notice your thoughts to be primarily positive or negative?
- Do you acknowledge your accomplishments?
- Are your thoughts overly boastful, demeaning or down to earth?
- Do you have thoughts of resentment toward others?
- Are you accepting of people's differences?
- Do you complain a lot about how people act?

When we bring our thoughts to the surface, now we can get curious about them. Do you really *hate* your sister, or perhaps you don't like something she did? We may normalize complaining as a pastime and something that people do when they get together, while later we understand how our complaining is draining our energy and turning us into a judgmental control freak! Catching ourselves in these moments is the first step to changing our thinking because consciousness is what allows us to build new pathways toward new thinking.

We're all human and have negative thoughts from time to time, but it becomes a problem when we have these negative thoughts about others and ourselves ALL THE TIME. Negative thinking, rumination, worry, or dwelling on negative events or emotions, can potentially consume more energy compared to positive or neutral thinking. Negative thinking can activate regions of the brain associated with stress responses such as the amygdala, a brain structure involved in the fear and stress response, as well as the prefrontal cortex, which is responsible for decision-making. Negative thinking can also lead to the release of stress hormones, which further drain our energy resources and contribute to mental and physical fatigue over time.

Next let's take a look at the thoughts you have about the world that we live in?

Fill in the blank:

I believe that the world is

____

The way children are being raised these days is

____

The most important lesson to teach our children is

____

- Do you think it's a "crazy" word, and no child should ever be brought into it?
- Do you think it's a dangerous world full of terrible people?
- Do you think your government is ruining your life, and that the world is unfair?

Maybe you don't carry any of those attitudes, but instead you see the world as a beautiful place full of experiences, dualities, and diversities to learn from. The truth is that the way you think forms your attitude → your attitude forms your belief systems →and your belief systems forms your reality.

In Napoleon Hill's book, *Think and Grow Rich*,[3] one of the top bestselling self-help books of all time, captures this lesson in the first chapter called, *Thoughts are Things*. He says, "whatever the mind of man can conceive and believe it can achieve". He highlights how common temporary defeat is in the process and not to let yourself become discouraged by it. Hill says, "Failure is a trickster with a keen sense of irony and cunning. It takes great delight in tripping one when success is almost within reach" because "success comes to those who become success conscious. Failure comes to those who indifferently allow themselves to become failure conscious."

This reminds me of a colleague who was trying to win a permanent position after being on contract for years. She was a very competent person, but when it came time to sit down for an interview, she had the belief that she was "terrible in interviews." Because of this belief she created her reality so that she would never get a permanent job. If you want to change your reality, you *absolutely* need to change the way you think.

Does changing your thoughts sound impossible? Of course not. But if you tell yourself that it is then that will be true. I love the quote by Henry Ford that says, "Whether you think you can or you think you can't - you're right"

Is changing our thoughts hard? For sure it is! We need to have an open mind to develop the mindset we want. This is an attitude of conscious awareness. The more you can shift your awareness out of negative, judgemental ways of thinking, the lighter you will start to feel. You will fill up with something that is opposite of judgment: acceptance. Acceptance of this moment; acceptance of yourself; acceptance of others; acceptance of the things you don't like; and acceptance of *all things* in general. Acceptance of the moment is a mindset as much as it is an attitude. Next I will give you a tool to use on a daily basis as your guide in changing your thinking.

2

The Four Mindsets:

The Mindset Tool Of All Mindset Tools

"The world as we have created it is a process of our thinking. It cannot be changed without changing our thinking"

ALBERT EINSTEIN

How do you change your attitude? By paying attention to your thoughts. This is THE WAY to becoming a more conscious thinker.

Changing Our Thoughts to Change Our Behavior

Cognitive Behavior Therapy or CBT, simply put, is becoming aware of your thoughts in order to change your behaviors and your life. Mental health struggles such as ADHD; Anxiety, Bipolar, and/or Developmental Disorders; Autism; Antisocial Personality, Borderline, and/or Narcissistic Personality Disorder, greatly impacts our ability to process our thoughts and behaviors in a functional way. Many of the clients I've worked with over the past few decades have been impacted by the effects of mental health and associated trauma and were the ones who needed CBT the most, but to have it work effectively required a degree of simplicity. Whenever I taught cognitive behavior exercises to clients in the past, it always seemed so complicated and ineffective. This was because it was never shown to me in a way that I could synthesize and share in a simple way. I didn't know why I couldn't wrap my head around the difference between feelings and thoughts-- plus having to understand the nuances of the situation that led to the behavior, was all very confusing. The mindset tool that I use with my clients today is one that is easy to apply and most helpful for those who are neurodivergent.

Our Thoughts Are Manifesting Our Reality

Since it is our thoughts that are directly responsible for our behavior, it is also our thoughts that are directly responsible for the reality we create. In March 2021, I took a masterclass with Bob Proctor, self-help author and lecturer. During his class, he clarified "The Law of Attraction" as a secondary law, and that "The Law of Vibration" is *the basic law*. In order for us to attract whatever it is that we want, we must be in the vibration associated to receive it.

The brain is therefore an electronic instrument, according to Proctor. What we think emits a frequency, be it positive, negative or neutral which will then lead to the attracted reality. In physics, it's been proven that our words and our thoughts are energy. Of course our feelings exist too--and guess what? Our feelings are influenced by our thoughts as well. So, I know I've said it a dozen times now: but to change anything, we have to change our thoughts first and to do that requires awareness.

How do we become more aware of our thinking? Below is the tool I teach my clients in my "Free To Be You Coaching: 8 Week Program" (Figure 1). It is such a straightforward tool that you can even teach this to your children. This model translates our thoughts in terms of colors. Using colors to describe our thoughts takes away associations with labels or clinical terms. We often associate colors with different moods and preferences, so I'll need you to put away those associations and develop new ones for the purposes of implementing this tool into your life.

There are four colors that I will speak about and each color relates to a different attitude. As you've come to learn, an attitude is a collection of thoughts. So as you read through the descriptions, you'll obtain a deeper understanding of how your own attitude can be characterized and understood.

As you read through each description, don't worry if you're not fully grasping them all right away. I will be generating plenty of examples and scenarios throughout this book so by the end you'll have a solid understanding of each color.

Are you ready to grow your self awareness? Great, let's get started!

GREEN
I COUNT/
YOU COUNT
WIN/ WIN
ASSERTIVE
RED
I COUNT/
YOU DON'T COUNT
WIN/ LOSE
AGGRESSIVE
BLUE
I DON'T COUNT/
YOU COUNT
LOSE/ WIN
PASSIVE
PURPLE
I DON'T COUNT/
YOU DON'T COUNT
LOSE/ LOSE
PASSIVE-
AGGRESSIVE

The Green Attitude

The Green Thinker is the watcher and the observer of the thoughts. The Green Thinker understands the principles of the "I Count/You Count" attitude. They always aim for a win-win outcome. This is a really important attitude to embrace, it's the most ideal actually, as this mindful watcher practices the observation of their thoughts. This type of thinking is always in the best interest of all, and most importantly--it strives to do so without judgment. Without judgment, however, is not the same as without caution. Whenever I speak of non-judgment, it is with respect to the attitude, not the behavior. One of the key features of someone with a Green Attitude is that they hold the belief that, "You are not better than me, and I am not better than you." Because Green Thinkers operate from this place of non-judgment, they have a good understanding of their personal and emotional responsibilities. This means that they easily respond to what they are responsible for and equally hold space for what they are not.

"Holding space" means allowing others to *be with* their problems and negative feelings, without thinking about how to fix them. Holding space is done by listening and asking questions from a place of non-judgement. This allows the person to feel heard and supported by you, instead of having their experience invalidated by you going into problem-solving mode. They will hold back on offering unsolicited advice and instead allow the other person to come to their own conclusions first.

This notion of holding space also relates to being personally responsible for your own thoughts and feelings. Green Thinkers know that they are responsible for their own thoughts and feelings. They will think twice before saying things like, "you *make* me so angry," or even "you *make* me happy." They have a keen understanding of the fact that it is *their own thoughts* that lead to their feelings and actions. Instead they would say *"I feel angry about what you did"* or *"I feel happy spending time with you"* This difference is because

Green Thinkers know that the thoughts, feelings, and actions of others are not their responsibility.

One of the biggest traits of someone with a Green Attitude is that whenever you have an interaction with them, they will never leave you worse off than when you found them. If anything, you'll feel better. That is because the Green Thinker exemplifies compassion, empathy, and a non-judgemental attitude. They exude an energy that is pure and authentic. You feel like you can be yourself whenever you're around a Green Thinker.

An example of this would be a Green Attitude who has been on several dates with someone, and although they got along well, they started to notice unhealthy patterns and values that were not in alignment with their own. As hard as it would be for the Green Thinker to tell them that they couldn't pursue a relationship, they would have to consider their own needs. Basically, in order to have a continuous cup running over, Green Thinkers have to make sure their source is clean and untampered with. For them, values in a relationship must come first.

Instead of dragging it out to "save" hurting the other person's feelings, a Green Thinker would be upfront and let them know in a positive, respectful way that these differences are not conducive to manifesting the relationship they were looking for. This is a win for the other person, because they were spoken to honestly and respectfully, and it gives them an opportunity to reflect on what they've been told. It's a win for the Green Thinker because they were being assertive, honest, and honoring their own valued needs. Non-judgment comes into play because there was no criticism of the other person and their irreconcilable differences. The Green Thinker accepts that we're all different, and in that regard they can choose which people will be part of their inner circle and which ones will not. That is how the Green Thinker is discerning and takes care of their own needs.

People with a Green Attitude take care of their own needs first, based on the "I Count/I Matter" attitude. They are also considerate of the needs of others through the "You Matter/

You Count" attitude. There is a fine balance, however, between counting the needs of others and being considerate of other people's needs, *versus* thinking that you are responsible *to meet* the needs of others.

In the example I gave about dating a person who compromises an individual's needs, had they chosen to stick around to help the other become more healthy, in the long run, this may have proven to not only be detrimental for themselves, but also for the other person, who may not have the experience of making changes on their own--if they wanted to.

When compromise needs to be taken into consideration, Green Thinkers know that compromising does not mean conforming. They would not compromise the important needs of their own for someone else as it doesn't allow for a win-win outcome.

The Red Attitude

The Red Thinker is someone that holds an attitude of being better than others. There is an attitude of superiority and entitlement. The Red Attitude thinks in terms of an "I Count/ You Don't Count" attitude. The "I Count" for the red is not the same as the "I Count" for the Green because unlike the Green Thinker, the Red Attitude does not consider the needs of others.

The Red Thinker is only concerned about getting their own needs met and struggles to show compassion for the needs of others. If they want something, they think they're entitled to receive it. Everyone has moments of succumbing to the Red Attitude, while there are others who spend the majority of their time operating from this way of thinking. If you happen to catch yourself in the Red Attitude and have this awareness, well then that is a very Green thing to do! But when the Red Attitude has been deeply ingrained and accepted, thoughts can turn to *manipulative* strategies. What this looks like is a fake "You Count," to others in order to win people over and get something from them to serve their own needs.

There's always the thought of, "What's in it for me" with the Red Thinker because they're more likely to do something for someone else if it will benefit them. For example, a seemingly goodwill gesture of helping someone move into a new house comes with a hidden agenda for the Red Attitude. They may not genuinely want to help with the move, but the motivating factor is to produce a deposit in the "relationship bank." Then when they want something from this individual later, they'll bring up the occasion, hoping they'll feel guilty for not making a return deposit into your "friendship account."

The Red Thinker can then become resentful and spiteful when their favors are not reciprocated. If you have a Red Attitude you may find yourself making your feelings the responsibility of other people. You may think, "If someone has made me angry, it's *their* responsibility to make me feel better." Red Thinkers will say, "YOU make me so angry." Or, "Look what YOU made me do." They'll also be the ones who say, "YOU make me so happy," while a Green Thinker *knows* that he or she is responsible for their own feelings, happiness included.

Let me further explain how being responsible for your own feelings works, because I know this can be confusing. Many of us were raised hearing the words, "you make me happy," and "you make me upset." We hear phrases similar to this in song lyrics and in movies that have normalized and contributed to the programming that has us believing that *other people* are responsible for how we feel--when in actuality, it's ourselves who are responsible for generating our own inner contentment, happiness, and sadness or anger. Seeing others as the source and responsibility of our feelings in the long term will only result in further disconnection from ourselves and an overreliance on others to validate our experiences.

Let's say I start showing up late to work as a result of staying up every night with a new love interest that ends up getting me fired. If I was operating from a Red Attitude, I would say "This new love interest made my life go off track and totally distracted me from my goals!" The truth is that it's not the love interest's fault that my life went off track, it was *my fault.* A Green response would be, "It was my decision to spend time with this person that later caused my life to go off track and distract me from my goals." The responsibility then becomes mine instead of blaming someone else for my behavior. No one causes us to do or think anything--we alone are ultimately in charge of that.

Another way to identify the Red Attitude is an obsession with winning and they don't care if winning comes at the cost of other people's needs. If you ever hear someone telling you "I just can't win with you" you might be showing up with a Red Attitude. Because the Red Attitude believes that their needs matter more than others, so they will go to great lengths to prove this, and ultimately win.

The Blue Attitude

The Red Attitude will often latch onto the Blue Attitude. Why is this? Because the Blue Attitude doesn't count themselves, a polar opposite to the Red. The Blue Attitude is one who thinks "I Don't Count/You Count." In other words, they don't consider their own needs, and they have a strong tendency to only consider the needs of others. They may not even think of their own needs at all and have an unhealthy focus on the needs of others. They believe that they are the cause of other people's feelings, especially the negative ones. If someone is upset, "It must be my fault." If someone's life isn't going as planned, "It must be because I wasn't there to give them enough support."

So you can see how the Red Attitude would latch onto the Blue Attitude because it supports the Red Thinking that: *other people are responsible for my feelings.* Those with a Blue Attitude are so focused on the needs of others that they put their own needs on the back burner as it's likely that they've been programmed to be more in tune with the feelings of others, thus they create codependent behaviors and toxic, one-sided relationships.

The interesting trend I've noticed when helping Blue Thinkers become more Green, they'll often overlook their Blue ways of thinking as Green. When they say they count others by being considerate of their needs, combined with the thinking that they count themselves because "helping others makes me happy," they find themselves fueling their happiness based on what they can do for others, instead of actually considering how to source that happiness internally. The Blue Attitude thinks that their self worth depends on what other people *think* about them. Getting our needs met from external sources is not only an unreliable source, it's also an inaccurate reflection of our *true self*. Self worth is something that is defined by you, not other people.

What ends up happening is a lose-win versus a win-win for these individuals. Blue Thinkers live in a world where it seems like everyone else gets what they want, while their own true innate needs are hopelessly unfulfilled. Blue Thinkers will be the ones to ask others, "Do you like me? Do you think I'm a good person? Am I doing a good job? Are you happy with me?" Many Blue Thinkers will indicate "I don't know what my needs are." While this thought is indicative of whether or not you are a Blue Thinker, it can also be a springboard into awareness, and in invitation to further investigate what that means for you.

The Purple Attitude

The Purple Attitude is beyond indifference. It's the, "If it wasn't for bad luck, I'd have no luck." "I can never catch a break." "Everyone is an idiot." Or, "The people who work here have no clue what they're doing." This is the "I Don't Count/You Don't Count" attitude. This one can be a bit harder to understand because of the lose-lose outcome involved.

Think of Eeyore from *Winnie the Pooh*. He's hopeless and

helpless with this "why bother/I can't win" attitude. Purple Thinkers lack assertive ways of communicating, but they won't be passive either. They want people to know how miserable they are and how inadequate everyone around them is. As a result, the way they communicate can come across as very passive-aggressive.

One thing I want to highlight about passive-aggressive communicators is that they are negatively sarcastic. They will pride themselves on their sarcasm without realizing how detrimental it really is to healthy relationships. The passive-aggressive approach is further normalized by the Purple Thinker by identifying themselves as a cynical person. They will make fun of themselves as much as they make fun of others; they are self-deprecating. They'll also rarely apologize for anything and don't care about making amends.

The Purple Attitude doesn't care if others understand them or not, because, "If you don't understand me it doesn't matter because I barely understand myself." This is where the "You Don't Count" attitude comes into play. They think, "I will never afford you a straight answer and I will make you read between the lines." Of course you'll notice this way of thinking in the Red Attitude as well, given the "you don't count" devaluing properties. However with the Purple Thinker, it's not to devalue or be deceptive, since they already devalue themselves as they may think, "What I have to say doesn't really matter anyway." Or, "What's the point in saying what I mean when no one cares?"

Ask them for a favor--and they'll immediately start telling you all of their woes and problems. They'll tell you if they did this favor for you, it would cause them actual harm and misery; it would be to the detriment of their day, week, month, or even their life, causing you to eventually say, "Forget it!" Purple Thinkers can also be quite indecisive as they don't care one way or the other how anything will turn out.

The Purple Thinker doesn't think anyone is capable of carrying out any task at the standards they expect, so they never ask for help and prefer to suffer instead. If they were to ask for help, it would never be good enough. The Purple Attitude thinks that the first step to failure is trying, so why bother? This is actually a very unpredictable place to be, and it is the only color of thinking that will result in suicidal behavior. In order to end your life you have to be in a position where you don't consider your own needs or those of anyone else. This is a very serious outcome of a lose-lose way of thinking.

It's Very Green To Notice When You're Not Being Green.

I want to highlight that *The Four Mindsets* is a tool that is based on a non judgemental framework. The absence of judgment is a crucial element in our capacity to learn new behaviors and subsequently find the drive to embrace transformation. It's a very Green thing to be able to catch yourself when you're operating from an insecure attitude, noticing in the moment that you're doing it, and then seeing how you may not have been counting yourself or counting others. From there you start to build a sense of conscious awareness of your thoughts and the confidence that at any time you can shift into a way of thinking that can serve you and others in a responsible way.

Bringing the Colors Together

Although our thoughts are often responsible for our feelings, the goal is not to change our thinking so we can feel better. The goal is to bring ourselves into a state of non judgemental thinking so we can achieve a state of neutrality. Much of what the Green Attitude embraces is neutrality, and at the very least this is what we are aiming for.

Dr. David Hawkins talks about the vibration of neutrality in his book, *The Map of Consciousness Explained*.[4] This is exactly the vibration we enter in the Green Attitude. He says that,

"People of neutrality have a sense of well-being; the mark of this level is a confident capability to live in the world." He adds that, "People at this level are easy to get along with and safe to be around and associate with, because they are not interested in conflict, competition, or guilt."

I want you to take some time over the next few days to notice the color of your thoughts. Pay attention and listen to the way in which other people are speaking. How people speak *is* an illustration of their thoughts. We cannot determine someone's character solely based on their behavior, as you will discover in the next chapter, however we can begin to discover clues about ourselves and others when we operate from this new awareness.

Return to the answers you provided in the questions in the previous chapter and see if you can determine what color your thoughts were stemming from. And remember, to do this review and reflection from the mindset of someone with a Green Attitude, one without judgment.

3

How Are You Being?

"Watch your thoughts, they become your words; watch your words, they become your actions; watch your actions, they become your habits; watch your habits, they become your character; watch your character, it becomes your destiny."

LAO TZU

Have you ever done something and then afterwards asked, "What was I thinking?" Or, "I don't know what I was thinking?" Or better yet, "I wasn't thinking?" The truth is that we are always thinking. It is said that we have between 6,000 to 70,000 thoughts a day. Whatever the number is, thoughts are always there and these thoughts are directing our behavior.

The work I did with those in conflict with the law required in-depth risk assessments in which I'd ask questions about family backgrounds, schooling, employment, substance use, mental health concerns, and of course what caused them to come into conflict with the law in the first place. Stories were either long and drawn out or very simple. I'd hear them talk about the build up leading to what happened, and how they spoke about everyone else's behaviors and what everyone else was doing, before I'd hear them speak about their own. There would often be a precursor to what happened with how life wasn't going so well for them, and how poorly they had been treated in their past, being victims of crime themselves. People would either minimize or deny what they'd done, or be in complete disbelief at how they even landed themselves in my office to begin with.

So if an individual is out there saying, "I don't know how this happened." Or, "How did I let this happen?," then they're a *human doing.* Human doings are not responsible, they are not conscious, and they are unaware. Human doings will risk their freedom, and then be confused as to how it could be taken from them. *Human beings*, on the other hand, are conscious. They take 100% responsibility for their actions so others can trust them, and more importantly--so they can trust themselves. Human beings have a sense of freedom, while human doings feel imprisoned.

If we want to become something else and stop doing the same things over and over that result in the same unfulfilled reality, we must step out of our *human doingness*, and into an empowered state of *being!*

An Attitude Is Not A Behavior

To be different, is to think different. And to think differently requires a conscious awareness of how you got there in the first place. The biggest takeaway from this chapter is that our behavior is a direct result of our thinking. To understand this in more depth, we'll return to the Four Mindsets and look into each through the behavior of lending money. All of the Four Attitudes will lend money, however each will have very different thoughts. On the surface, lending money to someone looks like a good deed; it appears that you are a caring, helpful person. However the *care* is more accurately captured by what you are thinking at the time. What are your intentions behind your behavior?

Lending Money From a Green Attitude

The Green Attitude will lend money when their thoughts are directing them toward a win-win outcome. They consider themselves and whether or not they can afford to lend money. They ask themselves if they will be in a tough position if they don't get this money back. In other words, can they afford to lose it? Then they have to consider the other person's needs as well. Remember the Green Thinker holds the principle of "I Count/You Count." They need to determine if this will result in a win for the other person, or if it will result in a loss. Certain things need to be carefully considered by the Green Thinker, so they aren't enabling someone else's harmful behavior.

They need to know what this person needs the money for, and if it's going to be used for something harmful or helpful. It's unlikely that the Green Thinker would even think to continue lending money to someone for a harmful purpose, even if this person always paid it back. This is because the Green Thinker knows better than to enable irresponsible behavior such as someone's irresponsible budgeting habits. The Green Thinker, although inclined to lend money when the factors were in line with their values, is unlikely to continue in this behavior over the long term as ongoing lending of money would become enabling.

Ongoing financial support outside of the Green Attitude may result in teaching others that "Anytime I need money I can just ask them for it, and they'll always lend it to me, as long as I pay them back." Or, "I don't have to budget myself properly. Instead I can just rely on them to help me out."

As someone who primarily operates from a Green Attitude, I have loaned a family member money, and they paid me back within a week of receiving it. This family member asked me again the following month for the same amount for the same reason. This time, though, instead of agreeing I told them that I was happy to help before, and I appreciated how quickly they paid me back––that this was a one-time thing. I told them not to expect me to get into the habit of lending money anymore. They respected my response and didn't ask again. It didn't impact our relationship either because of the way I communicated with them.

In working with one of my clients, she was able to stand up to a woman in her life using the Green Attitude and let her know she couldn't help her financially anymore. Surprisingly, the woman actually respected her more because of it! She told my client that she understood and was grateful for the help she had already given, noting that it was important for her to take responsibility for herself now. This client was able to turn a lose-win situation into a win-win outcome by not enabling someone else, which in return brought empowerment instead.

The Red Attitude Lends Money

Many people think there's no way a Red Attitude is going to lend money because they operate from an "I Count/You Don't Count" attitude. Don't be fooled by the Red Attitude wanting to help someone out. Remember, the Red Attitude is always about, "What's in it for me?" So the Red Attitude will lend money so long as it's paid back, but with interest or some other hidden manipulation or agenda to take advantage of the person. The Red Attitude also doesn't care what the other person needs this money for. It doesn't matter if they're going to use it for something that's harmful to them, because the Red Attitude cares only about how they're being seen by this act of "kindness." Behind the scenes there may even be threats or bullying to get the money back. The Red Attitude may request countless acts in return, because of the "good deed" they did for them. They also think much less of the person who needs their money and views themselves as a superior being in comparison.

I used to date a guy who would stop people on the street who appeared to be struggling with mental health issues and ask them if they wanted a few bucks. He'd get them to follow him back to his car, and then give them an over-the-top amount of money that they were not expecting. He would say afterwards that he chose that person to give to because "he wasn't asking for money or bothering people." He would even say, "I like to give *those people* money and help them out."

The intentions were to be perceived as someone who "cared" and was helping the "mentally unwell." His act of giving money was about feeding his own ego. He also left really big tips at bars and told me, "Now you can come back here anytime and be treated with the best service." He would only tip large because he wanted to be treated well the next time he went there, not because he really found the service to be outstanding.

The Blue Attitude Lending Money

The Blue Attitude, of course, will lend money--and will even borrow money from someone else to give it to you. Even though the Blue Attitude is "I Don't Count/You Count," it's still not of the mindset that they want *what's best for you*, rather they just want you to have whatever you need the money for *to be happy*. "Whatever makes you happy, even if I don't agree," is the Blue's plight. Whether it's to go gambling one last time, or to pay overdue bills that they've fallen behind on every month due to overspending habits--the Blue Attitude puts others before themselves to their detriment-- but for approval and to be loved.

This is where the Blue Attitude will mistake themselves for a Green Attitude through their acts of kindness. I've encountered this with many of my coaching clients who have an ongoing commitment to helping people in their lives financially. In these instances they are operating from a Blue Attitude and fear rejection or push back if they tell the person, "No."

Now you may be asking, "But what if they *do* get upset with me?" This is where we have to remember that we are not in control of other people's feelings. We have to know at the end of the day that we are acting in good faith, which means that we are acting with a Green Attitude. One of the hardest things for humans to deal with are the negative feelings in others, and we need to accept that It's okay for people to be upset with us. The Green Attitude would recognize that this person is stuck in a Red Attitude by blaming us for their problems. We can hold this Red Attitude with compassion, and understand that they are only capable of counting themselves right now, then let it go. Remember a key component of the Green Attitude is that they never leave anyone *worse* off than they found them. So either way, you're not robbing them of any money, you're not making their situation any worse. Enablement is what makes people worse.

The Purple Attitude Lending Money?

The Purple Attitude will lend money, but remember they want to make it a "I Don't Count/You Don't Count" or lose-lose outcome. How do they do that? With the intention of making you feel guilty for asking. Their thought is that if a person asks them to loan money, they will feel so bad about asking in the first place, that they won't even bother. There will be a self-loathing attitude about lending the money, and giving their last $100 to someone else would be a huge loss that would result in the other person feeling guilty for even asking. The Purple Attitude thinks, "How can they even have the audacity to ask me something like that?" While simultaneously thinking, "Fine, take my last $100, I'm probably going to wake up dead tomorrow anyway." Often the person asking will end up saying, "Forget it, forget I even asked."

There are many actions that get passed off as "acts of kindness." The problem is that we don't always see the intentions behind acts, or know what the person was thinking that got them to act in such a way in the first place. I know it's been said that actions speak louder than words, but I believe that our thoughts speak louder than our actions. The problem is that we don't get to hear the thoughts of others.

You can witness someone holding a door open for another person, and it likely appears that they are doing a kind act, meanwhile they're thinking, "Why am I always the one holding doors for people, when these people are so ungrateful, and no one ever says thank you? But here I am holding open the stupid door." What color attitude would you say that would fall under?

Don't assume, instead ask questions.

We are very quick to make assumptions about why people behave in a certain manner, so I will remind you that when you assume––you make an ASS out of U and ME! And it's true. I always encourage people to be curious and ask questions. This is the Green way to be. When you ask questions about your own behavior and the behavior of others, it holds you back from making judgements. Ultimately, it is the underlying mindset behind our actions that serves as the primary cause for why we persist in a particular behavior. Attempting to alter our behavior using the same thinking that led us to it initially will only have us returning back to the same patterns of behavior.

The Four Trauma Responses

Maybe you've heard of the Fight or Flight response, or the Freeze response? But have you heard of the Fawn response? The Fawn is just what it sounds like, "fawning" over someone and tending to their every whim. Also known as the 'friend and befriend' response, the fawner tends to the other's every need like it's their own, but with no regard for their own needs at all. Does this sound familiar? It's very much a behavior that stems from having a Blue Attitude.

These trauma responses are actually automatic reactions from the unconscious brain in response to perceived or real danger. To keep us safe, the nervous system shifts into a state of stress by releasing protective hormones such as cortisol and adrenaline. We needed these responses to keep us safe from saber-toothed tigers which the Fight or Flight response is very good at. When we wake up in the morning to go to work, our cortisol is supposed to be at its highest level for the day which motivates us to get out of bed and get off to work. It's likely our Fight and Flight responses are being activated a few more times throughout the day as we interact with the public or rush to meet tight deadlines.

In modern society, we no longer live with the threat of dangerous animals, but our brains are still responding to *perceived* threats in this same way. Over the course of history, our fears have changed. You might say that you have no trauma. You might say that you were raised in a home where your parents didn't hit you, in which you were provided for and had everything you needed. But what about your emotional needs? Were they validated, honored and understood? Did you have a caregiver that was distant, unavailable or unloving? How did they show you love? Did they tell you? Maybe they were financially supportive, but fell short in the emotional support department. You may have grown up in a household where you were expected to behave a certain way or you'd get in trouble, and/or seen as annoying or a nuisance. Maybe you were made to feel like a disappointment to the family if you weren't behaving in a way that was seen as favorable.

Some of us may minimize this type of invalidation by thinking, "It's just how it was." Or, "it wasn't really that bad." Or, "I'm fine." Other types of trauma that we may minimize are being in car accidents, losing your job, getting a divorce, experiencing a house fire, or a natural disaster. Maybe you were witness to your parents' hostile arguments or had a sibling that caused disruption in the home. You could've experienced the loss of a pet, or the death of a friend or family member. Trauma can also stem from being treated unfairly by teachers or authority figures, being cheated on by a partner or experiencing daily criticism from a loved one. The main factor when determining whether or not these experiences will result in the long term impacts of trauma is how you were emotionally supported during that time.

Dr. Gabor Mate talks about what trauma *is not* in his book, *The Myth of Normal.*[5] He says that it's not trauma if it doesn't leave you with limitations, or without diminishing your capacity to feel, think, trust, or assert yourself. It's not trauma if it doesn't leave you feeling overwhelmed and with the desire to escape through work or compulsive self-soothing or self-stimulating behaviors. It's not trauma if you're not left feeling compelled to justify your own existence.

If you've found yourself drinking too much alcohol every weekend for as long as you can remember, and often turn to substances to "make you feel better," or you drown yourself in work well beyond the point that everyone else has clocked out and left the office--then it's likely that you've got some unresolved trauma.

The Four Trauma Behaviors: Fight, Flight, Fawn, & Freeze

Let's look at each a bit deeper into these responses because no one is immune to experiencing one or all of these responses at some point in their life. The Fight response occurs when you get angry and respond to difficulties and stress through *physical aggression* toward yourself or others. You might yell a lot, throw things, punch holes in walls, and damage property. Maybe you grew up with someone who also behaved this way. If so, it was likely very confusing to understand, because the person yelling and acting aggressively towards you was actually reacting to their own trauma--trauma they never acknowledged or took responsibility for or sought healing to treat. Because of this, their trauma went on to traumatize others in their own life.

I'd associate the Fight response with the Red Thinker because the thinking behind this behavior is a self protecting "all about me" attitude. Or, "The world owes me" because I am a victim and must fight for justice. Or, "I'm the only one who knows what's right" which leads to many bridges being burned. At the same time, the Fight response can be helpful when you're actually fighting for your life or acting in self-defense. It then becomes, "I Count," for protecting yourself, as well as "You Count" by making the other accountable for their harmful behavior in a way that makes them physically stop.

Many world leaders over the course of history have been operating out of a Fight response when they engage in wars and human eradication. Consider it this way: people operating from a Green Attitude would never exhibit behavior that would result in a WWIII.

The Flight Response is much more common than we realize. It functions as the backbone of our work culture, encouraging people to use work as a coping skill and a way to avoid what's really going on in their lives. Being a workaholic is seen as a positive trait for many people, but in truth it's the opposite. Being a hard worker and putting in extra hours isn't being a dedicated employee--it's being a traumatized human desperately trying to avoid the depths, and pains of their lives by drowning themselves in work.

Yes, we need to work hard to reach our goals, but when it comes at the cost of others and/or yourself with no foreseeable end in sight, that's not strong will or determination, it's weakness and a showcase of self-abandonment. Self-abandonment is essentially a way for us to avoid ourselves. We avoid ourselves by invalidating our feelings. We avoid others by avoiding conflict and rejection which avoids opportunities for healthy relationships. The Flight response avoids asking for help, and avoids the present moment. The Flight response is on the go, and will do anything to avoid slowing down, because slowing down means they have to face themselves and face their feelings, which isn't something the Flight response knows how to do.

The Fawn Response, which I referred to earlier, is also motivated by avoiding conflict and becomes a mirror to what other people want them to be. Unfortunately this results in a loss of authenticity, because they'll always be wearing their people-pleaser mask. This can become quite exhausting, because they have to change their masks or wear more than one at a time. The Fawn Response can also occur due to having parents who were overprotective, overbearing, and/or over controlling. What we see from all of this is that our parents operated out of their own trauma responses, and then passed them down onto us.

These trauma responses have been so well ingrained into our DNA they become unconscious behaviors to us. We normalize them, and say "Everyone I know is like this." or "This is just how I am." But the truth is that just like learning any behavior, we can also unlearn these trauma responses. We can become more conscious of our behaviors by having a deeper understanding of the programmed thinking that has been feeding them. We can learn new ways of thinking and perceiving to develop a new belief system that will generate a healthier response. The Green Attitude is what gets us out of these trauma responses and into our modes of self-care, exercise, health and well-being.

Finally, we have the Freeze response. To illustrate the Freeze response, imagine that a big grizzly bear is running at you at full force! Do you try to fight it off, or do you take flight and try to outrun it? Maybe you play dead! This is exactly what the Freeze response does. We are responding to stress from the Freeze response when we zone out, tune out, numb out, or check out. A person who uses this response often may think, "Maybe I can become invisible to the world." A person in the Freeze response will literally feel stuck, paralyzed, or unable to speak. In my experience with the Freeze response, it's our body's way of preserving energy. For many who have spent years in Fight, Flight or Fawn, the Freeze response can feel like a period of dissociation, disconnection and disorientation.

These responses are all here for our human survival, and they serve us well in our lives--until they don't. Trauma responses stem from a brain region called the amygdala located in the old brain, and it's like the flame of a candle, shaped like an almond. The amygdala ignites and fires whenever there is danger, signaling your Fight or Flight response into action. If we were raised in chaotic environments, our amygdala was likely to fire all the time, and now as adults our alert systems are faulty and go off when there is no real danger present. Some may relate to the term hyper-vigilance, having an exaggerated startle response and overly sensitivity to loud sounds and large crowds.

The way to heal our nervous systems so we can function from a more secure place involves the practice of mindfulness. Being mindful in the present moment is the opposite of being in a trauma response and I'll elaborate on mindfulness strategies further along in this book.

4

How To Take 100% Responsibility For Your Life

"All blame is a waste of time. No matter how much fault you find with another and regardless of how much you blame him, it will not change you"

WAYNE DYER

The opposite of responsibility is blame. Whenever you're not taking responsibility for yourself, you're blaming it on someone or something else. There are various ways we avoid taking responsibility, and one of the biggest ones comes down to avoiding our own feelings. In an effort to make the uncomfortable feelings disappear, or to feel more comfortable the moment we turn to alcohol, drugs, over-the-counter medications, shopping, gossip, sex, or overeating. Instead of taking responsibility for ourselves, what we're really doing is creating long term habits of avoidance and the illusion of control.

If we never honestly face our uncomfortable feelings, they can't be processed in our physical body and instead they end up taking up too much space in our minds, causing overthinking. So, to be responsible for ourselves, we need to consider the question: *What is the intention behind my behavior?* Is my intention to connect with myself on a deeper level? Or is my intention to disconnect from painful emotions? A major factor in being responsible for ourselves involves the ability to self-reflect.

It was quite common in my work with the criminal justice system for clients to have a limited capacity for self-reflection. Those with a Red Attitude often fall into this category since they don't want to admit that they were wrong, and must continue with their illusion of always winning and being right. They're also the ones who won't want to become more self-aware or self-conscious because this is where the ego has to be put to rest for a while. For them it's much easier to find the flaws and mistakes in others.

To accept full responsibility for ourselves requires a certain level of willingness, as well as a conscious interest to grow our awareness from where it currently sits through the practice of non-judgement. In order to have the ability to respond without judgment, we need to have an awareness of our judgments. We can then consider how the Green Attitude would respond, and then move into a state of acceptance, which becomes our reminder to operate as a human *being*, instead of a human *doing*.

What Am I Responsible For?

There are many things that happen to us that we cannot control and that we are not responsible for, but what we do have control over, and what we are responsible for, is *how we choose to think about those things*. We can develop an understanding of how things are actually not happening *to* us, but *for* us. Everything is here for us to learn and grow from and within that are the teachings of personal responsibility. To help you obtain a better grasp of how to be 100% responsible for everything that happens to you--there are a few more concepts that I'm going to introduce you to. These concepts refer to how you view yourself and the world around you in terms of personal responsibility. Also highlighted is a reminder of what you are in control of, as well as what you can change and what is your responsibility and what is not.

What is an Inside Cue?

Inside cues relate to everything that is happening inside of us. Inside cues are our feelings, our thoughts and our memories. These are the things that constitute our *being.* Our feelings give us information as a cue to our thoughts, which may also arise as memories from our past.

We have *physiological responses* that are also cues, and clues us into what is happening within our thoughts and feelings. A pounding in our chest may be a cue that we are feeling anxious or nervous. Or it may be a cue that we are having thoughts about the future or pending doom. This physical discomfort may cause us to take a deep breath and go to a quiet place to feel more calm. Or this cue has us seeking immediate relief through one of those distractions I mentioned above.

A headache is another cue that sparks a feeling of physical discomfort, or irritation. From there our thoughts might tell us that we're possibly dehydrated, so the body sends this message to drink more water. Or our thoughts may tell us to get rid of this pesky headache with some other remedy like taking ibuprofen. When we realize that we are responsible for these inside cues, we take action to resolve them. The level of attention we give ourselves, depends on the level of personal responsibility we are willing to take.

Being in tune with our inside cues is personal responsibility in its highest form. Our inside cues are the thoughts we have about everything that is happening both inside and outside of ourselves. It's therefore our responsibility to catch those thoughts, before they find us in behaviors that we later regret. Catching ourselves in a non-green thought, allows us to take responsibility for ourselves by making adjustments to our thoughts, which then affects our feelings and subsequent actions. Thoughts and feelings are your responsibility. You are in control of them, and you can change them. Thank goodness for that!

What is an Outside Cue

Meanwhile, outside cues are not in our control, we are not responsible for them, and we cannot change them. If inside cues are the things happening inside of us, then outside cues are all the things that happen outside of us. I'll break those outside cues into these three categories:

People
Places
Things

Things refer to smells, sights, or sounds. It can be a text message or a post from someone you see on social media. It can be the rain, the sun, or a pipe that suddenly springs a leak in your basement, that then cues a thought, a feeling or a memory. As mentioned at the start of this chapter, the things we consume to avoid taking responsibility such as alcohol, drugs, over-the-counter medications, shopping, gossip, sex, and overeating, are also outside cues. We engage in utilizing these things as ways to avoid our inside cues.

We also do not have control over other people. Now some of you may disagree and say, "But, some people *are* my responsibility." Of course if you are a parent you may think that your three-month-old baby is your responsibility, and yes there is that. Some may say that their thirteen-year-old teenager, or their aging mother with dementia is also their responsibility. At the very least I want you to consider that *the feelings* of a three-month-old, a thirteen-year-old, or an eighty-year-old--are *not* your responsibility.

If we have said or done something to them that wasn't motivated by a Green Attitude, we can notice our default, take responsibility by apologizing, and making sure it doesn't happen again. However none of that guarantees a shift in how that outside cue will respond to us. Our thoughts may tell us, "Ok I've made peace with them now so they ought to feel better" and the point I'm highlighting here is that their response depends on their inside cues and whether they choose to feel better or not.

Having a Green Attitude means that you understand that you are not responsible for the inside cues of others, and that you are only responsible for your own thoughts, feelings and actions. If someone has a meltdown, is crying inconsolably and even raging, then I would argue that it's okay for them to do that, as long as they are not harming anyone else or themselves in the meantime.

The Green Attitude would not enable a thought, feeling or behavior in someone who is causing harm to themselves or others because the Green Attitude operates from a place of compassion and genuine empathy.

Reframing your 'Triggers'

The term "trigger" is often used to describe something that elicits a strong emotional or psychological response in an individual, typically due to past trauma or distressing experiences. Some argue that relying too heavily on the notion of being triggered can shift the responsibility for managing one's emotions onto external factors, rather than taking personal ownership and developing coping mechanisms.

Advocates for removing the word "trigger" from our vocabulary suggest that by reframing our language, we acknowledge our internal, emotional responses and actively work on addressing and managing them. This can involve cultivating self-awareness, seeking appropriate support, and developing healthier coping strategies.

However, it's important to note that the concept of triggers is still recognized and valid in many therapeutic and mental health contexts. Triggers can be real and impactful, and for individuals with certain conditions, understanding and addressing triggers can be crucial for their well-being.

These outside cues are commonly known as "triggers" in our society. We've heard the word thrown around for some time now. You hear, "You triggered me." Or, "I got triggered." Or, "That's a huge trigger for me." The problem with this word as it's used in the examples above is that it takes away from our own personal responsibility, and puts the blame onto something outside of ourselves. A "trigger" goes against the teachings of what an outside cue is, which is something that is not in our control, is not our personal responsibility, and is often something that we can't change. Remember what you can change, though! Your inside cues!

Things you may hear yourself saying about outside cues that alter your view of
responsibility:

- "If you weren't late, then I wouldn't have gotten so upset and yelled at you."
- "If it wasn't for that social event tonight, I wouldn't have had so much to drink."
- "Because you cheated on me, I threw all of your clothes in the trash."
- "Because my dad was never in my life, I've always dated unavailable men."

- "Because my boss fired me, I can't get another job."
- "If you disrespect me, I will disrespect you back."
- "If you made me upset, then I will seek revenge."

What you'll notice here is the tendency to point the finger at others to explain our behavior. These thoughts take away our personal responsibility and rob us of our own inner authority while also holding us back from living healthier and more productive lives. Blaming others for our life circumstances is actually what keeps us feeling insecure and powerless.

While you are not responsible for outside cues, you are responsible for *how you choose to respond to them*. How you choose to respond is your responsibility. They are synonymous. Just look at that word responsibility: *response* plus *ability*. You have the ability and the responsibility to respond from a Green way of thinking.

Let's say you have a history of social anxiety, and attending crowded social events tends to *trigger* feelings of discomfort and insecurity. Without acknowledging our own role in managing our feelings of anxiety by developing coping strategies, we might blame the trigger, crowded social events for our behavior by saying something like, "I was shy and standoffish at the party because the large crowd triggered my anxiety." In this example, the focus is primarily on the external factor, the large crowd, as the main cause of your behavior. When we give power to the outside cues, we lose our ability to take responsibility for ourselves.

When we don't take responsibility for ourselves, and we don't consider a Green way of thinking about how to attend a crowded social event, it makes sense that it would result in feeling insecure and uncomfortable. Green Thinking allows us to take a compassionate view that understands we are sensitive to being in crowded spaces and will need to set up some limits and boundaries for ourselves, instead of feeling limited by things we don't have control over.

If I've convinced you to minimize the word "trigger" from your vocabulary then I want you to replace it with the word *cue* instead. When we refer to all of those things outside of us simply as a *cue*, we make ourselves responsible for how we choose to respond to those cues. It's a reminder to slow down, take a breath, and check in with your thinking before you determine how you are going to respond. Outside cues are always here to remind us that regardless of what is happening outside of us, we are always responsible for how we choose to respond to it internally. Even if it takes a while.

Practice makes progress, not perfect!

Perfection is never the goal for the Green Attitude. Instead of focusing their attention on perfection, they focus on the progress they've been making toward their goals. This is what fuels their determination and motivation to make life a practice instead of a performance. We all have to allow for mistakes and errors, and understand that human behavior will include misbehavior or folly. That's because everyone is *practicing*. No one has it all figured out and even when you think you do, a new challenge will come along to bring you back into a state of practicing and learning.

Many perfectionists I know not only hold themselves to high standards, they hold others to unattainable standards as well. Perfectionist attitudes may think that outside cues are within their control and this is why the perfectionist will never achieve a win-win outcome. It's easier to blame, shame and complain about what other people are doing, or not doing as the reason why we're not experiencing our own progress. Perfection ultimately leads to fears such as a fear of failure or a fear of making mistakes. A perfectionist may therefore find it difficult to take responsibility for their mistakes which inhibits their ability to learn and grow. If someone who carried a perfectionist attitude were to admit their faults, it may confirm that they are unable to meet the high standards they have set for themselves. On the other hand, perfectionists might overcompensate for their fear of making mistakes by taking on excessive responsibility for things that are beyond their control. Ultimately this behavior can lead to burnout, undue stress and overwhelm as they try to maintain control over everything.

I've noticed that perfectionism is also linked to procrastination which often leads to giving up on the thing and never seeing it through to completion. Many perfectionists I know commit themselves to unrealistic deadlines that later contribute to their delays and to feelings of overwhelm when they can't make good on their promises. If you identify with being a perfectionist, it's helpful to remind yourself, 'Done is better than perfect.' No matter how long you try perfecting something it will never be 100% perfect, especially for the perfectionist! Getting things finished then becomes more important than endlessly striving for perfection.

Which Mindset Blames Others?

The opposite of responsibility is blame. Whenever you're not taking responsibility for yourself, you're blaming it on someone or something else. When we blame others for our actions, this is the epitome of being an unconscious human. The Purple and the Red Thinkers play the "blame game." They don't take responsibility unless it serves them to do so, especially the Red Thinker. The Purple Thinker is constantly criticizing and complaining about what's wrong in the world and uses these injustices to explain why they're not able to live the life they want, while making no effort to do anything about it. The Purple Thinker is perpetually caught in its own trap of lose-lose. They don't want to see anyone legitimately be successful, nor can they grasp their own ability to be successful given their inability to be responsible for themselves. This results in a victim mentality, which all non-green thinkers are susceptible to.

Having a victim mentality is a common mindset flaw that we can all be susceptible to from time to time and if we spend too much time there, we'll end up losing our power and ultimately our inner authority to be responsible for ourselves. A client of mine who came into the Free To Be You coaching program was at a standstill in her relationship with her aunt, and thought she wouldn't be able to move on until she got an apology from her. It took a few sessions and a few email exchanges before she came to the realization that an apology was not going to be the answer. She told me that she realized she was operating from a place of victimhood and by applying the Green Attitude she was able to call herself out on her judgements. She was judging the way her aunt had handled things after her fathers death and as a result wasn't able to access any of her father's belongings or keepsakes.

She sent me an email after a few weeks of trying to sort this out for herself saying her aunt was actually a good person who did a *"bad thing."* After this breakthrough, she said she could feel the pain that she'd been attached to for so long finally leaving. Her aunt's actions no longer felt personal, which allowed her to forgive her aunt, neutralizing the problem and was ready to reconnect with her again from a better place. Initially she felt like this injustice was happening to her, but in the end it was happening *for her* to see how her failure to take responsibility for her own thoughts and feelings was holding her back from having a relationship with her aunt.

Dr Hawkins writes in his book, *Letting Go*, "We are free to hang on to negativity as long as we want. There is no law that says we have to give it up. We are free agents. But it makes a big difference in our self-concept to realize that 'I won't do something' is quite different feeling than to think that I'm a victim and I can't."[6]

Which Mindset Blames Themselves ?

The Blue Attitude feels responsible for everyone other than themselves. They take responsibility for how other people feel, act and think. Feeling responsible for yourself as a Blue

Thinker feels selfish, while feeling responsible for others actually turns out to be a form of control. This is why it's so common for Blue Thinkers to want to fix people, and make them feel better. This is a very difficult habit to break and is often part of a learned behavior called codependency.

Codependent behavior is common for those operating from a Blue Attitude as they often have an exaggerated sense of responsibility for the well-being and happiness of others. They may feel a need to control or manage other people's actions, believing they are solely responsible for ensuring that everything goes smoothly, and when it doesn't this leads to feelings of guilt and self-blame.

Which Mindset Operates From The Highest Form Of Personal Responsibility?

The Green Thinker knows that they are only responsible for themselves and that it's selfish to make others responsible for them. The Green Attitude takes responsibility for their own feelings, challenges and struggles and that taking responsibility for themselves is a sign of self-respect.

When someone has disrespected the Green Attitude, they don't see it as their responsibility to correct the other person. The person who behaves in a disrespectful manner is first "dis"connected from their ability to respond. The level of personal responsibility that is required in the face of a perceived disrespectful person, is of the highest level. Hence, it's best to be an observer in these instances and hold up a mirror for self-reflection because someone else's disrespect of you is not your responsibility. This comes back to understanding that they are an *outside cue*, and you are not responsible for outside cues. You only need to be responsible for observation.

The Green Thinker is going to observe from a place of non-judgement. As they observe this behavior in others, they observe the effect that this disrespectful behavior is having on them, instead of absorbing it as a personal attack. It's quite natural to be offended by someone's disrespectful behavior, so if you can catch this reaction in yourself as it's taking place and respond with compassion and non-judgement then you've brought yourself into alignment with a Green Attitude.

The Green Attitude doesn't need to ever take on the responsibility of another human, unless they have been given consent to do so. Even then it is not wise to fully be in control of another human, because taking responsibility for someone else means you have taken control of them. Once this valuable lesson is realized, there will be a lightness, a weight that has been lifted from holding onto this unnecessary responsibility just so you could feel needed, valuable, and worthy.

When I finally took 100% responsibility for how my life was going is when I felt like a liberated woman. I was able to take responsibility for a marriage that wasn't serving my needs. I took responsibility for my own financial success. I took responsibility for how I wanted to be treated, and I took responsibility for the life I wanted to live.

When we were younger our caregivers held the responsibility of teaching us how to take care of our emotional needs by offering us praise, providing feedback, and holding us when we would cry. Whether our parents did that for us or not, as adults it's now our responsibility to do these things for ourselves. If these qualities of affirming your worth were not displayed consistently or at all in your fundamental years-- then being responsible for ourselves becomes even more difficult. Learning to do this work for ourselves and showing up for our own needs sounds daunting, so no wonder we find it easier to focus on the needs of others instead.

Sadhguru, head of the yogic Isha Foundation in India, writes in his book, *Karma*[7]:

Once you understand that you are one hundred percent responsible for your life, you will naturally choose to live consciously, rather than unconsciously. An unconscious life will not unfold the way you want it to. A conscious life, on the other hand, will unfold in the best possible way for you. Your karma is not in what is happening to you; your karma is in the way you respond to what is happening to you. Your suffering is not because of your circumstances. Your suffering is because of the way you have made yourself.

The Difference Between Independence and Hyper Independence

If you've made it this far in the book --then you are someone who is ready to take responsibility for yourself and you can start to adopt this new belief: *I am solely responsible for meeting my own needs.* One thing to watch out for however is becoming too independently responsible.

When we take on all the responsibilities we become *hyper-independent* and become too self-sufficient which creates a different kind of insecurity. Hyper-Independence thus stems from a Red Attitude, thinking no one is capable of helping us, and we discount our need to connect with other humans. We are then forced to rely solely on our own insecurities to get it done. Cue the perfectionist thought pattern, "If I want it done right, I have to do it myself" because there's no room for mistakes. Another one is "It's faster and more efficient if I do it myself," because collaborating with others is perceived as time consuming, or that others won't fully grasp the outcome they want to achieve. Finally this is one that many Blue Thinking perfectionists will find themselves saying "I don't want to be a burden or inconvenience anyone" which supports their reluctance to impose on others' time, efforts or resources.

Sometimes this insecurity will come from a distrust in others, or being too rigid in wanting to do things our way as we stay closed off from new ways of doing things. We need to be cognizant of this, so that we can reach a level of *interdependence*.

Independence Vs. Interdependence

Independence emphasizes self-sufficiency, autonomy and individual decision making. Although the independent person seeks support and input from others, they ultimately make decisions and take actions on their own. Interdependence on the other hand emphasizes cooperation, collaboration and that we are interconnected beings. Interdependence is also the opposite of codependency.

A hallmark of the Green Attitude operates in this interconnected, interdependent fashion. They know that although they can do many things on their own, they also know that asking for help, connecting, collaborating and seeking support with others is a responsible thing to do. To think that you can do it all--all by yourself--without any help, is irresponsible. Green Thinkers acknowledge that while individuals are capable of doing things on their own, they are comfortable to receive help and share resources to achieve common goals. It's important to recognize the strengths and contributions of each person because this is how we can enhance our collective experiences and generate positive outcomes.

5

How Validation and Invalidation Influences Our Behavior

"Because one believes in oneself, one doesn't try to convince others. Because one is content with oneself, one doesn't need others' approval. Because one accepts oneself, the whole world accepts him or her."

LAO-TZU

Internal and External Validation?

What is more important, internal validation or external validation? Just like outside cues, outside or external validation isn't something that we have control over. If we're constantly doing things to obtain outside validation, it will become an unsustainable and unreliable way to operate. It would appear then that the validation we give to ourselves becomes more important, and the external validation we receive serves to support the internal validation we've given to ourselves. Meanwhile, we need to ask ourselves who's in control of my internal validation? We are! So why don't we reward ourselves more often? Collectively as humans, we seem to be much better at internally devaluing ourselves before anyone can get a word in edgewise. We're always the first to criticize and beat ourselves up and may even close ourselves off from receiving external validation.

When we operate from a Green Attitude we can honestly validate and invalidate ourselves based on a balanced and compassionate set of beliefs about ourselves. Being able to validate ourselves is what helps us to build confidence and self-esteem, as our self worth is being generated from within. With a strong ability to validate yourself, comes a decrease in the need for opinions or approval from others, and when they do come, because they will -- you'll meet them without judgment. The Green attitude recognizes the judgment in others, and can normalize that we all judge from time to time. It's an experience that we find neutrality in and acceptance so we are not allowing ourselves to be susceptible to the negativity from others. Repeat after me: "I am not responsible for outside cues. I cannot control outside cues. I cannot change outside cues. I am only responsible for how I will choose to respond to them"

While it's important to find a balance between internal and external validation, internal validation serves as an anchor in times when external validation is lacking or is unreliable. And don't think I'm totally knocking external validation either. External validation can provide a sense of belonging and reassurance as well as serving as a valuable tool for feedback, motivation and learning. It's just not meant to be the main source of our self worth and self esteem.

How To Change Unwanted Behaviors

Working for twenty years in the criminal justice system I learned that not everyone will respond in the same way to imposed consequences. Let's say you went into a store, stole a chocolate bar and walked out without being caught. From this experience you'd learn that stealing chocolate bars is a behavior that you could get away with, and so you might go back and steal again. Someone who behaves in this way is likely operating either from a Red Attitude, which would have them stealing for their own benefit. Or a Blue Attitude, who would steal for someone else and was willing to pay the price of getting caught to please them. What if the Red Thinker did get caught? They might think, "I need to get smarter and steal from a different store." The only outcome that getting caught produced in their behavior was that they needed to be smarter about stealing. As they moved on to steal bigger ticket items, the Red Thinker says, "That's what their insurance is for." Or, "They're already making enough money, and this one loss won't affect their business." Now they're full of cognitive distortions including minimizing and justifying, so they can continue with their behavior instead of acting in a less harmful manner.

The Red Thief

For the Red Attitude in this case, a healthy level of internal invalidation, in the form of facing harsh truths about oneself would need to be present and would carry more weight in changing their behavior than external devaluation would.

That's why a cheating partner doesn't just stop cheating because they got caught. Instead they just get smarter about it.

I was taught as a probation officer that it wasn't recommended to focus on building self esteem for someone with a Red Attitude and what would be more helpful was teaching them to have compassion for others. Typically there would be little to no interest for them to engage in such a thing. They might give me some acknowledgement of compassion or empathy at first, but quickly enter into blame, shame and devaluation of everything else. These were tricky conversations to have with the ones who were on probation for domestic assault. I would often wind up being devalued along with everyone else if I wasn't careful in my approach. Even with a careful communication style, having these types of conversation around compassion and empathy for Red Thinkers is next to impossible.

I had one of them honestly admit "you can't expect that from me" in response to whether or not they could have compassion for someone. For a Red Attitude to move into a Green way of thinking they must understand the unhealthy ways they validated themselves, which was in conflict with the well-being of others. The validation a Red Thinker can give themselves for assaulting someone is the feeling of power and control. This is validating for the Red Thinker and will lead them to behave this way again as they got a huge reward from it. Power and control are not rewards for a Green Thinker, especially when it comes at the cost of someone else. Power and control are not even viewed in the same way by a Green Thinker who sees power in kindness and control in their own behavior.

The Blue Thief

The Blue Attitude will do anything to receive external validation from others, even at the cost of their own freedom. For the Blue Attitude to change their behavior, instead of focusing on punishing their behavior, they need to focus on increasing their self-compassion. This is also what will allow them to also become more Green in their thinking. When the Blue Attitude hears parents, teachers, classmates, or friends devaluing them, *they believe it* to be true, and as such will shape their behavior to become what they think others think about them. This is especially true when they don't have enough external validation to counteract it.

If the Blue Attitude's behavior of stealing was rooted in rationalized thoughts of needing to provide for someone else--such as stealing food to feed their children, or while under the influence of a Red Attitude, the outcome of external validation from their children who are now fed and feeling happy, and from the person who pressured them to steal, may lead them to continue with this or other illegal actions.

The external validation they received for stealing might teach them to continue this behavior, but once someone with a Blue Attitude is caught, this would likely fuel their low self-worth even more. External devaluation for the Blue Attitude exacerbates their own internal devaluation, resulting in feelings of toxic shame and guilt. Because they've done something wrong, that means to them that something is wrong with them. This could lead to further incidents of stealing or unlawful behavior, since they're seen as a "bad person" anyway.

What is clear is how ineffective punishment can be for someone who is insecure and likely why the sentencing aspect of the criminal justice system fails to teach people how to become more prosocial.

For someone who was a first time, low risk offender, it was recommended that they came into the office for meetings as minimally as possible, and in some cases I would remove this requirement altogether. What we found was that by continuing to have someone attend an office that was associated with punishment would increase their risk to reoffend. Why was this the case?

These low risk clients felt nervous sitting in the waiting room alongside "hardcore criminals". Some would make a point of telling me "Look, I'm not like them." It's possible for us to shape new beliefs about ourselves based on our behaviors.

People-Pleasing

What is the thinking behind people pleasing? You may have said something along these lines:

- "Other people's feelings are more important than my own."
- "To put my needs ahead of theirs is selfish."
- "They can't do anything for themselves."
- "Who else will help them?"
- "When other people are happy, I'm happy"

People pleasing is a behavior that is externally focused, and seeks external validation. There is a lot of energy exerted in this behavior as it also has to avoid criticism and external disappointments. As a child, people-pleasing may have brought you much praise; perhaps it turned you into a perfectionist, and you may have achieved a lot of success in life because of this. You possibly entered into a field of work which involved solving difficult humanistic problems or helping people in their personal life. You are naturally a very nurturing and caring individual who is involved in the "helping" professions, like nursing, counseling,social work, animal care, or teaching.

While your validation from others is teaching you to continue as a people pleaser, negative external responses leave you feeling confused and hold you back from behaving this way again. The people-pleaser then conforms to how others want them to behave and they put on their own sort of mask, that is different from the mask of the Red Attitude. The people-pleasing Blue Thinking mask is worn to keep the peace, while the Red Thinking Mask is worn to later disrupt the peace.

Everything we do is done in order to meet a need for ourselves. When I say "everything" I mean *everything*! We behave in specific ways to meet our need for food, shelter, safety, security, acceptance, respect, and a sense of belonging. For the people-pleaser, their behavior is meeting the need to be accepted, to be liked, and to be perceived in the best light. The Red Attitude doesn't care to be liked or to be accepted, they just want what you have and if they can't have it then they'll move on. Being liked and accepted is important to the Green Attitude as well, however it's more related to a sense of self-love and self-acceptance which then extends to all with compassion.

6

Insecure Attitudes in Relationships

It's important to be aware of the primary attitude you've brought to your relationships so you can reflect on how they've impacted your behaviors, so you can now take responsibility Being in a relationship is indeed a behavior that we all perform on different levels, and just like anything else, bad habits can form when it comes to how we relate to others. To give you further insights into your habits as well as others, I'll break down a few examples of how each color attitude may conduct themselves in a relationship along with what possible thoughts are influencing their behaviors. I'll also tie in the associated trauma responses so that you can start to see how all of these pieces fit together.

Dave & Suzy

Dave has been *collecting* thoughts and *programming* his belief system for the last thirty-seven years, resulting in the development of a primary Red Attitude. He was raised by a codependent mother who was always trying to protect him from hurt feelings, disappointment, and frustration. If there was ever a problem at school which caused him to feel sad or upset, she would come to his rescue to make him feel better. If Dave was unhappy, his mother would go above and beyond to cheer him up. In this way, his mother was teaching him that she was responsible for his feelings. Dave's mother has always been very uncomfortable with negative emotions, so she felt it was her job to put on a happy face for her son every single day.

Dave was a risk-taking kid, and as a teenager he became a rule breaker, as he'd often stay out beyond his curfew. He would hear his mother say things like, "You are going to give me a heart attack." Or, "If you keep this up, I'm gonna lose my mind." These comments were laughed off and disregarded by teenage Dave. He lacked the ability to see how his behavior could possibly impact others, but at the same time, he was especially good at holding other people accountable for how they behaved towards him.

Dave's father was the breadwinner of the family. He felt that as long as he was financially supporting his family, there wasn't much else for him to do; his role was being fulfilled. Dave's father worked out of town a lot and was barely around. His father struggled with alcoholism, and although Dave's father would never consider himself an alcoholic--he relied on alcohol as a coping skill to avoid negative feelings and to handle stress. His father's behavior in this way would be seen as responding from the Flight response.

This was a behavior that Dave's father learned from his father, and one that Dave would also utilize down the road. Using alcohol, or other substances including food, is a common behavior that will occur in families who see difficult emotions as negative, and something that needs to be ignored, denied, and pushed to the side. Coping with negative emotions by numbing and devaluing them has already been normalized by the generations before Dave, making the pattern even more difficult to break.

His father's maladaptive use of alcohol was a source of stress for Dave's mother, as it had him spending more money than they had. Dave's mother was responsible for the household while he was away, and she rarely called upon her children for help. This further contributed to Dave's conditioning, that he wasn't required to be a responsible member of the family, and that the only one who was responsible for everything--was his mother.

One night Dave overheard an argument between his parents in which his mother was questioning his father about sleeping with another woman. Dave's father's typical response to these accusations was to tell her that she was insecure. He'd also ask infuriated, "Why do you always have to ruin our time together by bringing this up?" Dave heard his father yell, "You're probably the one cheating on me while I'm away on business! If I ever find out that you have, I'll kill you and your idiot lover!"

What Dave witnessed growing up between his parents resulted in the belief that it was other people's responsibility to take care of his needs, even when his behavior had been terrible. He would sometimes take on a victim role and need someone to rescue him, just like his mother did for his father all those years. Along with Dave's risk-taking behaviors, alcohol use being one of them, he had a hard time maintaining full-time employment and would often take under-the-table cash jobs or sell drugs on the side.

Dave complained about his bosses and hated working for "the man." He refused to take responsibility for his own actions and preferred to place blame on everyone else instead. After years of a terrible credit history from credit card debt, bankruptcy became the only option for him. Since he didn't have any assets, Dave figured it would be easier to declare bankruptcy than pay back his debts.

Dave learned from watching his father what it took to get what he wanted through skilled manipulation tactics. He understood that if he put on a fake persona, the one that made him appear as though he was interested in the needs and interests of others––this would position him as a "desirable" man. Although Dave felt superior to others, he would portray himself as less than superior in order to get what he wanted. This deception would give him an ego boost, seeing how easily people could be taken advantage of, and more importantly, the validation he gave himself for being so good at it.

Cue Suzy whom he meets at a New Year's Eve party. Suzy is the one who loves to fix, save, and rescue others as a way to validate her self-worth. She learned from her parents that being nice is her very best quality, and that it's more important to be nice to others than toward yourself––because being "nice" to yourself is selfish. Suzy had a very similar upbringing to Dave's in that they were both adult children of alcoholics with codependent mothers. Suzy had adopted the conditioned beliefs of her mother: *that her worth was based on what other people thought about her*, and what she could do for others mattered more than what she did for herself. She believed that doing for others was what made her happy. As a result, she'd developed an insecure attitude and often responded in behaviors from the Fawn trauma response.

Dave knew that he needed to approach her in a certain way, by giving her the impression that he thinks she's great and that she is the superior being! He is immediately drawn to Suzy and offers to buy her a drink while showering her with over-the-top compliments on her outfit and "perfect body." As you have learned, the Blue Attitude bases their self-worth on what other people think about them. Because Dave does this so well, Suzy will immediately be drawn to his compliments. Once he finds out that she's single, he'll pretend to be in shock and ask how someone like her doesn't have a boyfriend.

Consider for a moment how someone with a Green Attitude would approach someone who caught their eye. Their actions would be predicated on a genuine respect for personal boundaries. They would likely make an effort to introduce themselves first, instead of complimenting the person's physical appearance. The benevolent action would be to ask questions in order to get to know the person of interest better.

Unfortunately, instead of seeing these gestures and comments as red flags, Suzy soaks them up and immediately begins to fall for Dave. Meanwhile, Dave continues to test Suzy's boundaries to see just what he can get away with. He buys her another drink, then puts his arm around her waist--which she allows. Dave suggests that they leave the party to go hang out at his place for the rest of the night, which would mean she'd have to leave her friends and be without support. When Suzy agrees to come home with him, he knows that his manipulation is working and confirms that she is the easy prey he thought she'd be.

Within a few days, Dave starts asking favors of Suzy as he talks about his struggling business, and how crazy his ex-wife was, who "took everything" from him. Next, he'll find out what Suzy's good at and create a deficit about himself in this area. Maybe she has a housecleaning service, so he'll tell her he really needs a housekeeper. Or maybe she's a teacher, so he'll tell her that his son could really use a tutor. Suzy thinks this is a great way for her to connect with someone through her skills, because she loves to help and will rarely say no as a fully operating Blue Attitude.

Suzy's Blue Attitude will become exemplified when she tells Dave that he doesn't have to pay for her services. Even if he offers to pay, she won't make a big deal about it one way or the other. At first accepting payments from him would make her feel like she's taking advantage of him, but over time she'll start to feel like she's being taken advantage of, because she is. Suzy believes that if she stops tutoring or house cleaning, Dave won't like her anymore and will leave.

This will result in putting her hopes and dreams on the back burner and giving up the hobbies she once enjoyed. Just as she ditched her friends the first night she met Dave-- she will grow further and further away from healthy support systems.

Since Dave behaves from a Red Attitude, he wants Suzy to only consider *his needs*, and this is exactly what the Blue Attitude is conditioned to do. Dave perceives loyalty in a relationship as someone who unconditionally takes care of his wants and needs. If he sees her tending kindly to someone else, he will get incredibly jealous. The Red Attitude thinks that if you are giving someone else attention, there will be none left for them, so they have to make sure that they have you all to themselves. Developing secure attachments is not what the Red Attitude has been conditioned to do. They're conditioned to feel insecure in their relationships as children, and without a secure and loving adult, they will not grow out of this. Later as adults, the people we choose to have relationships with either help or hinder our recovery from these insecure attachments.

When the Mask Comes Off

It won't take long for Dave's Red Attitude to rear its ugly head. Just a few months into the relationship, he'll start to slip up and talk about other people in a rude manner. He'll speak negatively about the waitress at a restaurant, and how she needs to lose weight because her clothes are too tight. Later

Dave will complain about the dinner she made him and then brag about what a great cook he is. Suzy will start to question the stories Dave has been telling her about "his crazy ex-wife" and will have her eyes more open to his disrespectful comments he keeps making about her. After a few more incidents of Dave showing disrespect toward women she'll start to get annoyed that he keeps playing a victim and blaming his struggles on the ex. She starts to shake her head and no longer thinks that Dave just needs a good woman in his life. Suzy starts to realize that she needs to get better at choosing better men.

The Shift Out of Blue Thinking

Suzy has been with Dave now for almost 2 years and as she approaches her fortieth birthday, she's feeling weighed down, tired and burnt out. Like any thought that pops into our heads, we don't always take action on them right away. Suzy's thinking had shifted back to, "He's actually not that bad." and, "Other women probably have it worse, I just need to be grateful that I'm not alone anymore"

She's gained some extra weight and hasn't been as active as she was before she met Dave. Dave doesn't compliment her like he did when they first met, so she also feels less attractive. She is starting to realize how distant she's become from her friends and family, as well as not being as productive at work. A lifetime of being a helper to others has become unfulfilling and unreliable. No matter how hard she tries to please others, it still leaves her feeling *unworthy*.

As someone who operated with a Blue Attitude, Suzy held the belief that she was responsible for how other people felt, as well as thinking she was responsible for their problems. Letting go of being responsible for others is terrifying for her, because her entire self-worth has been built on a foundation of *what she can do for others*. Similar to Dave, she is also dealing with a fear of abandonment, and this she starts to wake up to. There may be different catalysts that show up to help her shift into a heightened state of awareness about her behaviors. Maybe she'll come across someone in her Instagram feed who says something that sparks a new perspective. Or she picks up a new book that encourages her to reevaluate her life and recognize the habits that have been keeping her stuck. Whatever appears in her life, it will have done so because deep down she's wishing for a real change. She scours through videos on-line and starts to feel validated by hearing about other women who are going through similar experiences.

Over the next few months she can feel herself stepping out of an old skin and into a new way of being. Suzy decides to hire a personal trainer and starts going to the gym three days a week. She also begins to reconnect with her friends and family. It's hard for her to make these reconnections, but something inside is telling her that *this is what she needs to do*. Suzy is no longer validating Dave's woes as much as she used to, and isn't taking responsibility for his feelings and needs as much as she used to. Instead of being bombarded by constant complaining from Dave all the time, she's beginning to open her mind to a freer and lighter way of thinking.

When Dave finds out that she's been spending money on a personal trainer, and that her weekend is not open for them to spend time together--alarm bells begin going off in his head, and his insecure attachment rages to the surface. Dave begins to realize that something is changing and he tries everything he can to throw her off course. His Fight trauma response is cued and he attempts to influence a change in her behavior by invalidating her. As we learned earlier, external devaluation, and invalidation is extremely detrimental for those operating from a Blue Attitude. Knowing how this works, Dave devalues Suzy by telling her that the personal trainer must be the worst one in the gym as he doesn't notice any improvements and that she's still fat. Instead of Dave moving out of his Red Attitude and telling Suzy how great it is that she's making this time for her family and friends, and more importantly--for herself, he begins to accuse her of lying. He doesn't believe that she's actually spending time with her family and that instead she's been cheating on him. Not only does this devalue her and the changes that she's making, it also devalues her friends and family.

Another low will be when Dave accuses Suzy of her parents never liking him, and that her mom was always so rude to him. "Why do you care about them anyway?" he'll ask. "You know, I'm all you need!" He'll tell her that he can't stand her friends, and then he'll make her question if they're even real friends at all since she's spent so much time away from them recently anyway. "They're all fake friends," he'll try to convince her. " I'm the only person in your life that even cares about you."

At any point when the Blue Attitude starts to count themselves by setting boundaries and taking care of their own needs first, instead of others, the Red Attitude will devalue the Green Attitude to try to bring it back to Blue. This is a very important stage to note for a Blue Attitude who is actively shifting into a more Green way of thinking. It is of massive importance that they know there will be consequences from the Red Thinkers in their lives. This is also a time when the rose colored glasses are taken off to reveal the red flags the Blue Attitude had been blind to.

Dave has no clue how to give himself love, approval, validation, or acceptance since he learned how to make other people responsible for all of these things. Suzy knows that remaining in an insecure environment with Dave will slowly erode her efforts to empower herself, and Dave isn't showing any signs of taking responsibility for himself any time soon. As Suzy shifts out of this "I Don't Count" attitude and into the "I Count/I Matter" way of thinking, she will need to be supported by her environment. It's very difficult for people to experience personal growth in the same environment that contributed to their decline. Being around positive people who are not judgemental is essential to opening her eyes and seeing Dave's true colors. The most important thing she'll learn from all of this is that it's okay to put herself first.

What will inevitably follow will be a "make it or break it"

period. Will she stay on her new self-empowerment path, or will she feel too much guilt and shame for taking care of her own needs and revert back to her Blue Attitude? Regardless, Suzy will learn that with every step forward she takes, there may be a few extra steps back. The more she focuses on moving forward into self-love, the more she'll stay true to her path and not allow any setbacks to discourage her.

If Suzy is successful in moving herself more and more into a Green Attitude and makes the Green choice to end her relationship with Dave, she will do it in the most compassionate way, by utilizing the "I Count/You Count" attitude. She will not highlight his deficits, criticize, or blame him in any way. Instead she will 100% take responsibility for how she got there in the first place. Finally she will graciously wish him well as she moves forward into a more positive life, all while Dave is left feeling very confused about what just happened.

Introverts & Extroverts

Let's begin with a definition of what an introvert is. Sometimes we mistake an introvert for someone who likes to be alone, but it's more than this––it's about energy. An introvert is someone who recharges their energy by being alone. For example, if an introverted person has been at a large social function for several hours, they will feel immediately drained once they get home. They will probably need a day or two to recharge their battery by spending time alone before being able to socialize again.

Extroverts, on the other hand, receive their energy from being out and about and around other people. They feel energized going to social events and can carry on in this fashion for hours and hours. For this reason, extroverts typically prefer being around people rather than being alone. However, it is a myth that we are either purely an introvert or purely an extrovert, because the truth is that it is very rare to solely be one or the other. The majority of us, at 80%, are ambiverts.

This means that we need to experience a bit of both extroversion and introversion to recharge our social batteries, but that balance may look different for everyone.

For me I can say that I'm about 70% introverted and 30% extroverted. After being alone for too long, I know that I need mental and emotional stimulation by being around others. If I ignore that need, then I may start to feel sluggish. This sluggishness, or low mood, is linked to how we get our energy. This need for stimulation could even just be about going to the gym, or a coffee shop and *being around* other people, but not necessarily interacting with them. Many introverts prefer the company of nature or animals to humans, and so they need to honor this need within them as perhaps an unconventional external source of energy.

Is there a relationship between the Red Attitude being more extroverted and the Blue Attitude being more introverted? I would say yes. The Red Attitude gets energy from attention from others, so they will seek it out. The Blue Attitude innately gets their energy from time spent alone, but they rarely honor this quality in themselves because they are always trying to fulfill others' needs. This is because they also need external validation to define their worth.

It's within the Green Attitude where a person comes to recognize a healthy balance of time for themselves and time with others. From the Green perspective, the need to extrovert oneself doesn't come from the need for external validation, but rather to validate what they already know within themselves. Extroverted activities are therefore seen as a valuable way to experience healthy connections, enjoy shared experiences, and improve energy levels. Conversely, introverted activities from a Green Attitude is seen as necessary for the preservation of energy and personal alignment instead of being seen as a recluse or as an act of lonely isolation.

It's quite common for individuals to form relationships with those who possess contrasting energies. I'll often hear about extroverted partners who effortlessly engage in social interactions, relieving their quieter counterparts. However, issues arise when our partners fail to comprehend our preferred methods of recharging. The insecure introvert may see their extroverted friends as a threat or intimidating, while the insecure extrovert may view introverted individuals as cold and standoffish. This underscores the importance of looking for those green flags that signal respect and consideration from a Green Attitude.

Rohan and Anna

Let's delve into the story of Rohan and Anna, both introverts who were brought together through mutual acquaintances. Rohan and Anna both have a history of being in unreciprocated relationships, and their friends couldn't believe how similar their background stories were. They thought they'd make the perfect couple, because they were so much alike. In their previous relationships, they were both constantly criticized and made to feel that they were always being "too sensitive" and "clingy." Neither of them knew how to assertively express their needs, so whenever they'd try to get their needs met, they were told they were being unreasonable. Through experiencing this invalidation of their needs, they came to believe that their needs didn't matter.

For their first date, Rohan invites Anna over to his place so he can make her dinner. He feels most comfortable in his own home, and that security ensures that he'll really be able to impress Anna. Anna admittedly wasn't sure if it was a good idea to go to someone's house for a first date, but because Rohan had glowing reviews from his friends, she decides to trust the group and accept his invitation. Although at first Anna wasn't used to someone cooking her dinner and being so genuinely considerate, they both end up having a great time.

Anna really likes how easy going Rohan is and how he never argues or gets upset with her. For the first time in years, Rohan doesn't feel like he's walking on eggshells anymore, as he had felt in his previous relationship. With Anna everything seems to be flowing nicely and he tells his friends how they never argue about anything. When couples say, "We never argue," this is a possible indication they are both operating from a Blue Attitude. Two Blue Attitudes don't argue because they don't want to experience conflict. They have a negative association with conflict, which in the long term will breed resentment. An interesting fact about resentment is that it's hidden anger and so is jealousy.

Rohan works for the city's water department and Anna is a teacher. Both pride themselves in the work they do and always aim to please their bosses and coworkers. Anna goes above and beyond for her students, and Rohan takes on extra duties and responsibilities when the city becomes short staffed. The dating couple continue to see one another, and after a few years they plan to buy a home together. Once their first child is born, Rohan and Anna stop giving to each other, and instead put all of their energy into their children. Since they are operating from a Blue Attitude, Rohan and Anna often put their children before one another.

If you ever hear someone tell you, "My children come first," this most likely stems from a Blue Attitude. It's much healthier, and safer to follow the instructions given to passengers flying with children: to give *themselves* the oxygen masks before their children, because you can't help anyone if you've run out of oxygen. Anna and Rohan were losing the life-giving force of "oxygen" that the relationship required in order to sustain itself.

Like most first time parents, their first child became the focal point of their existence. Couples who operate from a Green Attitude know that by tending to the foundation of the child's support system, they will yield a much healthier upbringing for their kids. Putting ourselves first creates a balanced and sustainable approach to parenting that benefits everyone in the long run. Due to the inherent characteristics of Blue Thinking, Rohan and Anna would care for their daughter in a manner that aimed to fulfill her desires, making efforts to ensure her happiness and shield her from any disappointment or frustration. Meanwhile, Anna was burying her frustration and disappointment with her unmet needs that she was unable to express.

After their daughter turned four years old, Anna and Rohan welcomed a new addition to their family, a baby boy. They had taken into consideration the opinions from others, that it was selfish to raise an only child and that they must give their daughter a sibling. This put even more pressure on the couple and they started to count each other less and less. It was very important for Anna and Rohan to be seen as perfect parents, and as a result held very high standards for how they parented their children.

Despite all of the parenting books that Anna has read, she still doesn't see herself as a good mother. She often feels anxious and nervous about not being able to meet her children's needs. She questions if she's doing enough, and despite how hard she tries--she's always doubting her abilities and feels as though her efforts are never enough.

Rohan feels like he just can't be *man enough* for Anna. He hopes that by working hard and taking care of the household finances and home repairs, is enough to satisfy Anna's needs. Anna struggles to express her feelings and doesn't want to complain, so she continues to stuff her feelings away. She also doesn't think that there's much anyone can do to help her so she suffers in silence. Since Rohan also can't communicate his feelings to Anna he has started to work even more hours and is now turning to food as a way to cope with his insecurity. What's happening is that both Anna and Rohan's inability to value their own needs has landed them in a negative situation. As they grow further and further away from themselves, they create a bigger divide between one another.

Anna starts to notice her resentment toward Rohan who has been working more overtime than usual, and spends the rest of his time in the garage tinkering with his car and other motorized toys. She notices her resentment is also building toward her students who have started to become *too* dependent on her, and she has not been able to set healthy boundaries with them.

Rohan finds it very difficult to discover his role in the family because Anna does it all. Once in a while Anna will blow up at Rohan and tell him that he needs to help out more with the kids. Usually this ends with Rohan saying, "Just tell me what you want me to do." And Anna telling him, "Nevermind." This leaves Rohan feeling confused, and matters remaining unresolved. Neither of them know how to discuss their problems or seek out any support. Instead they stay overwhelmed and resentful.

Anna takes advantage of Rohan's absence because while he's in the garage she can have a few glasses of wine to help her cope with her overwhelming feelings of anxiety. Her body responds with odd illnesses which over the next few years the doctors can't explain or seem to pinpoint. When she confides in her friends, it's only to express her concerns about Rohan and how she thinks he might be depressed.

Anna's parents aren't very supportive and over the last four years have only been to visit their grandchildren on holidays and birthdays. When Rohan's parents visit from out of town, Anna treats them like houseguests, cooking and entertaining them the entire time, leaving her *even more* depleted. It seems like everyone else is getting what they want, except for her.

What they don't realize is that they're raising one child with a Blue Attitude and another with a Red Attitude. The oldest daughter has grown quite entitled because what she asks for, she gets. Anna and Rohan don't want to see their kids upset, so they do whatever it takes for them to stay happy and content. Any time their daughter cries or complains, they fix it right away. Meanwhile, their youngest son never asks for much, and he caters to everyone's needs as well. If he's hungry, he makes himself a snack. If he's bored, he just finds himself something to do or play with on his own. He has learned from watching his mother to never ask for help and to always do things for himself.

What I often notice with two Blue Thinkers in a relationship is that eventually when one of them decides that the way they've been living their life has become unmanageable resulting in a willingness to *count themselves*, what ends up happening is that instead of shifting into a Green Attitude to count themselves, they adopt a Red Attitude. This is where the resentment that I spoke about as hidden anger comes to the surface again, which can act as a significant catalyst because conflict finally has a space to arise. This may be the turning point that one of them suggests counseling. For Anna and Rohan to successfully turn this ship around to greener pastures, both partners will need to face the harsh truths about how their Blue Thinking has gotten them into this mess. Similar to Dave and Suzy, both of them need to be willing to make the changes together otherwise, one will ultimately be left behind.

The Insecure Red, Blue and Purple Relationships

The Red Attitude and Blue Attitude are a common dysfunctional relationship, as are two individuals with a Blue Attitude. Two Red Attitudes, on the other hand, is not as likely. This may manifest as a one-night stand, or a very casual relationship in which neither person seeks to satisfy the other person's needs long term. Two Red Thinkers are both playing each other's game, and it will be very short lived, or as an "on again/off again" type of pairing. We hear about these types of relationships where one person is only with the other for their money, for sex, or as "arm candy." These would be the only reasons two Red Thinkers would stick around each other for any amount of time. Remember the Red Attitude is about "what's in it for me," so as soon as something isn't serving them, they'll start to look elsewhere.

There will not be a deep sharing of emotions between two Red Thinkers, except for in the beginning when they were both very charming and over idealizing one another, as a way to ensure they would both be getting what they wanted out of the relationship. There may be infidelity on both sides, including secrets and skeletons that could come out of the closet at any moment.

It's also unlikely that two Purple Attitudes will end up together either. The Purple's emotional unavailability stems from thoughts that they don't take themselves or others seriously. The Purple Attitude hardly cares for their own wellbeing, nevermind caring about the wellbeing of another individual. Since the Purple Attitude is stuck in a freeze response, if a relationship was established, they may not acknowledge it or have fallen into one by mistake.

A Green Attitude will not engage in a relationship with someone who displays a Purple Attitude. This is because the Green Attitude will quickly be able to recognize that this other person doesn't count themselves or others. The Green Attitude would likely repel the Purple Attitude away, being seen as "too good for me" or "too perfect" or "too good to be true." The Blue Thinker would have this attitude as well.

7

The Secure Green Attitude

"I can do nothing for you but work on myself and you can do nothing for me but work on yourself."

RAM DASS

Erik and Lewis

Erik and Lewis didn't start out as Green Thinkers. Lewis was very much struggling with a Blue Attitude when he first met Erik. Lewis had a history of relationships with people who were takers and manipulators, and Lewis was always left feeling taken advantage of and a doormat. You could say that Lewis was a people-pleaser.

Erik was operating from a Purple Attitude in his earlier years and didn't have a good memory of his childhood or his teenage years, because he learned to disassociate, zone out, and feel out of his body most of the time. In his 20s he shifted into the Red Attitude as a way to feel better and "count" himself. This resulted in him holding other people responsible for his feelings as he hung onto his victim mentality. Erik used to blame others for how he felt, and didn't care to discuss his feelings, because he didn't think that anyone listened to him anyway.

When Lewis met Erik, he was ready to be in a serious relationship and knew this was his opportunity to finally practice setting boundaries in a healthy way. For their first date, Erik invites Lewis over to his place for drinks. Erik's response is to suggest meeting in a mutual, public spot instead. They have a fun night, and then hang out a few more times after that. Each time, though, Lewis realizes that all they're doing is drinking together. Lewis knows that this is not how he wants to build the foundation of a healthy relationship, so he tells Erik that he enjoyed the time they spent together, but that it isn't going to be a good fit for him.

Erik is heartbroken as he was genuinely starting to develop feelings for Lewis. Erik reflects on what has happened, and realizes that he has some bad habits that he wants to change and hopes that maybe Lewis will reconsider. Lewis is hesitant at first, but after seeing how motivated Erik is to live a healthier life, he decides to give him a second chance.

Together they decide that they will stop drinking for a while. This results in a joint love for an alcohol-free lifestyle.

In order to bare their souls and be authentic, they both had to get out of their comfort zones to show a level of emotional vulnerability. This was something neither of them had done before. Although they were both in their early fifties, they felt like they were in their twenties again, but this time with much more *self-awareness*.

They begin to count themselves in ways they hadn't before. Erik is choosing a healthier lifestyle--not just so Lewis will have a relationship with him--but so that he can be *happier with himself*. This was the kind of partnership he truly wanted to offer Lewis. Lewis has started to count himself in a way that he hadn't been able to either. For the first time in his life, he isn't going to bend himself to be what someone else wants, just so he can get their love and affection. Instead he's going to speak up about what his standards are, and if someone wants to join him with this same attitude, then it was definitely someone worth his time! In order to break the unhealthy relationship cycle of Lewis' life, he becomes comfortable saying "no" to a potential partner whom he really likes--but who isn't going to be good for him in the long run. Amazingly, counting himself has actually *brought* love into his life.

With Erik and Lewis we have two people who came together with one being very sure about the direction they wanted their life to go--and the other in a state of standstill or limbo. As you've come to learn, one person operating from a Green Attitude can have great influence on others whom they come into contact with. Their intention is to allow others the opportunity to decide for themselves what direction their life will take, while simultaneously not leaving them worse off than when they found them. Luckily, Erik was motivated and willing enough to make a life-changing decision, which seemed to come out of nowhere.

Lewis and Erik are now learning how to be more conscious thinkers, and to let go of the goal to be perfect. Even though there are arguments, there is respect for the other's boundaries such as no name-calling, no bringing up the past, no yelling, no threats to leave, and the option to take a time out if necessary. Not only do Lewis and Erik give each other empathy and compassion for these things, they also *give themselves* compassion when dealing with less than ideal emotions.

As a result, they both understand that healthy conflict is important for the growth of a lasting relationship. If one partner isn't taking responsibility for their unhealthy behaviors, this could be due to a Red Attitude. They both have the ability to recognize when one of them starts to slip back into their insecure attitudes, and then work together to come back into alignment. They know how to respectively call the other out on behaviors which may be a result of Red or Blue Thinking. They relate to one another in a non-judgemental way and show compassion for the other's shortcomings. There is a loving patience now, and a deep understanding that change takes time.

A responsible partnership means that both parties take care of themselves so that each can offer the other the best of what they are capable of. The goal is to *cater your connections to match the life that you want to create for yourself.* Noticing the attitude that others project is not the easiest thing to do, but now that you have The Four Mindsets to guide you, you'll be able to notice the subtleties behind the behavior of people we interact with regularly.

The Green Attitude Does No Harm

Let's take the example of a partner who doesn't want to quit smoking. Quitting smoking is a very difficult habit to break. There's a saying that comes to mind about quitting smoking, "Quitting smoking is easy, I've done it a thousand times." We notice people making changes to harmful behavior, but then it's often short lived. It's short lived because of the mindset that was driving the change in behavior.

If the change in behavior comes from a Blue Attitude, for sure it won't last because they're only counting their partner's needs, while secretly missing the stimulating effects of nicotine. They haven't accounted for how they will consider themselves in this process and so they revert back to the attitude that allowed them to continue smoking in the first place.

You might guess the thinking behind a harmful behavior toward oneself is going to fall under the Blue Attitude, and initially this is where it starts, but in the long term the decision to continue this unhealthy behavior comes from the Red Attitude.

The sneaky thing that makes this a Red Attitude is that by not making this change to their unhealthy behavior, they still expect this person to stay in the relationship despite the harm that it's bringing to them as well. Of course they could consider the other person by not smoking around them to eliminate the harm caused to their partner. However, as the years go by the person who continues to smoke might have health issues that result in leaving their partner alone one day.

The Red Attitude considers their own need to continue smoking because otherwise they'll be depressed and end up eating more resulting in weight gain. They'll say "You don't want me to gain weight do you?" or "You don't want me to be irritable and depressed, do you?" While that may happen, there's also a level of personal responsibility that is missing with the Red Attitude. The ego is working hard to maintain this attitude so that it won't have to face everything else that needs to heal alongside their addiction to nicotine.

The Green Attitude knows to give themselves the best opportunity to mitigate the harms that are brought into their relationships. When we operate primarily from a Green Attitude, we won't engage in toxic, harmful activities, which is also considerate of others because they benefit from us being at our best!

The Relationship Teeter-Totter

The teeter-totter images below provide further illustration to help us understand the relationship dynamics of what it feels like being in a relationship with each of the 4 Mindsets.

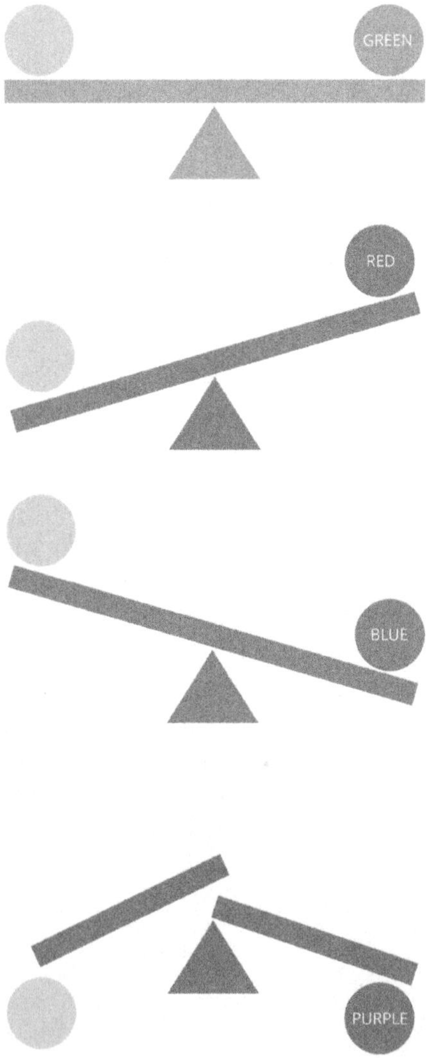

- The Green Teeter-Totter goes up and down on each end with equal effort. Both riders share the role in creating a balanced and respectful relationship. They both put in the same effort to create balance as they work together to create a win-win outcome.

- The Red Teeter-Totter only allows one person to enjoy the ride. They expect the other person to do all of the work as they hold a sense of entitlement to have things done for them. The Red Attitude isn't interested in bringing the other person up at all, which results in a win-lose outcome.

- The Blue Teeter-Totter works hard on the low end to make sure the person on the other side is always up. They give them the best seat, while their end may not be as stable or secure. They work hard to give the other person what they want, and are often making many repairs to the teeter totter at their own expense, which is a major loss for them.

- The Purple Teeter-Totter is broken. No one gets to ride it because no one is making an effort for it to work. They've given up. It's a lose-lose scenario.

8

Feeling Your Feelings

If thoughts are things, then feelings are information.

Our feelings are the messengers that provide invaluable insights into our experiences, perceptions and overall well-being. By embracing our feelings as valuable information, we can deepen our self-awareness, foster self compassion and authentic connections with others. Our emotional states are a rich tapestry of information that colors our lives, inviting us to explore and understand the depths of our human experience, while providing us with a wealth of data about our experiences, desires, and needs.

Try this quick exercise: Place your right hand on your heart, take a deep breath as you close your eyes, and as you continue to breathe into your heart space, tune into four feelings you're having right now.

Did you do it?
Could you come up with four feelings?

It's okay if you had a difficult time with this. Maybe you noticed a few things, but were not sure if they were actually feelings? Maybe you connected with bodily sensations instead. If you are someone who lives in your head all the time you will have a hard time accessing feelings because you've learned how to intellectualize feelings instead of actually feeling them. The irony is that you can't truly *think* about your feelings, you have to *feel* them first--then the mental processing comes later. Others may have learned how to be in tune with the feelings of others, instead of their own, which has them taking on the emotions of others as if they were their own.

Let's dig a bit deeper here and ask yourself the following questions:

1. When you cried as a kid, how did your parents respond?
2. When you expressed your feelings, how were they received by your caregivers?
3. Did you feel safe to express your emotions?

If you were told:

- "Stop crying, or I'll give you something to cry about."
- "Stop your crocodile tears."
- "This is not worth crying over."

Then your feelings were invalidated.
If you were ever told:

- "Stop being so dramatic."
- "Oh, you're just being too sensitive."

Then your feelings were invalidated.

If you were not allowed to get angry, told to "get over it," or "it's not a big deal," then *your feelings were invalidated*. If you constantly heard, "Well, at least you didn't have it as bad as I did when I was your age." Or, "At least you still have a roof over your head." Or, "You should be grateful for the things you have," then your feelings have definitely been invalidated.

As a result of these invalidations, you've been programmed to tell yourself that your feelings don't matter. If your feelings don't matter, then how can you, as a human, matter? This leads us to feelings of unworthiness and toxic shame. When we lack the ability to show up for our own feelings and validate our own worth, we'll continuously suppress our feelings. You might hear people say that you need to "sit with your feelings," but you probably just want them to go away because you're not used to acknowledging them.

Dr. David Hawkins says in his book, *Letting Go*, "Handling an emotional crisis leads to greater wisdom and results in lifetime benefits. Fear of life is really the fear of emotions. It is not the facts that we fear but our feelings about them."[8] Would you agree? Isn't the tough stuff really where the most growth and enlightenment come from?

What Would Each Of The Colors Think About Their Feelings?

Anger

Let's start with the feeling of anger. You might not think that the Green Attitude gets angry, but of course they do. The difference is in *how they think about that feeling*. The Green Attitude understands that anger is an emotion, just like any other emotion, and they tend to it with *compassion*. They know that *the thinking* behind their feelings will lead them toward an action of either tending to their feelings with care, or ignoring their feelings altogether.

The Green Attitude will validate their anger by giving themselves permission to feel it without judgment. The last time I got angry, it was because someone was projecting their anger onto me! I was upset because of their projecting! I was upset that this person could not come to understand me from a Green Perspective. In response, I acknowledged my own anger. I allowed it to have space for a period of time. I cursed, I felt the tension in my body, and I even felt like having a glass of wine to make the feeling ease up! Instead, I sat with it for a while longer.

I asked myself what it was that *I needed*. I needed some fresh air, so I went outside. I needed to process what was going on, so I journaled about it. Then I needed to shake it off, so I put on some music and moved my body through the emotion of anger. I reminded myself that I am not only responsible for my actions, I am also responsible for my emotions.

The Red Attitude believes that others are responsible for their feelings, so if I'm feeling angry and I blame my anger on someone else, this is a cue for me to see how I've entered into a Red Attitude. You can certainly catch yourself saying, *"You* make me angry," by transforming that into, "*I* am feeling angry in response to something you said or did." The Red Thinker may turn their anger into joy by seeking revenge against someone else because they think the way to feel better is to bring someone else down who did them wrong.

The Blue Attitude will want to *repress* the feeling of anger. They might tell themselves that it's unhealthy to be angry, and that anger is a useless and negative emotion. The Blue Thinker may experience shame if they allow anger to arise. This can cause them to feel quite unstable and unsafe, so they shove it down. Most of the time, Blue Thinkers experience an extension of anger in the form of resentment. The Blue Attitude is more likely to bypass their anger for self-pity in order to match the general view of themselves that "they don't matter." They don't see any value in expressing anger, because "no one will listen to them anyway." Their anger is frowned upon, and they believe it will get them into trouble. So, it's best just to bury it.

The Purple Attitude doesn't like to think about feelings at all. The Purple Attitude prefers not to experience feelings. They prefer to be in a state of dissociation and to not take anything seriously. They believe that feelings are useless and serve no purpose. Any attempt to express feelings will be done in a passive-aggressive manner. There is a disconnect between their thoughts, feelings, and behavior. The feeling of anger is denied, even though their behavior may still be reflective of it. The Purple Thinker might even speak in an angry tone, but then they will deny what they're feeling is anger. Remember, the goal for the Purple Attitude is "Lose/Lose," or "I Don't Count/You Don't Count." They deny themselves connection to their feelings, just as they deny others the opportunity to connect with them. Because they've already given up on hope, faith, themselves, and others, the Purple Attitude can be an unpredictable energy to be around.

All of these colors, except for the Green Thinker, are acting in a *protective* way. They are trying to feel safe and secure amidst unsafe and insecure feelings. The safety they seek is by not feeling or by shifting the feeling onto someone else.

For the Green Thinker, emoting is an opportunity to look deeper, stay present, and enter into a state of acceptance of their feelings. It allows them to check in with themselves, and to take time to contemplate right action, or what needs to happen to bring harmony and alignment. This is where emotional immaturity shifts into emotional *responsibility*.

When anger arises you can ask yourself:

"Do I need to take a break from this activity or conversation?"

"Do I need to journal about this experience to gain further clarity?"

" Do I need to go outside for a walk to clear my head?"

"How can I take responsibility for myself at this moment?"

In Dr. Paul O's book, *You Can't Make Me Angry*, he talks about the negative ways in which we react to other people's behaviors. He references the Al-Anon saying, "Don't complain and don't explain." He says that this is especially true when it comes to our feelings. "You feel the way you feel because that's the way you feel. No one said feelings have to be logical, and you don't need anyone's permission to feel them."[9]

There is a big difference between saying, "*You* made me angry," and "*I* am feeling angry." In fact, I suggest that we avoid saying, "I am angry," in general. We do not need to identify with our feelings in this way, because they don't define *who we are*. In one moment, I may feel angry, but that is not who I am. In another moment, I may feel sad, but that's not who I am either. By changing the language in this way, we allow ourselves to be open to experiencing *all feelings*, without attachment to them.

Happiness

The Green Attitude welcomes the feelings of happiness and joy with gratitude. The Green Attitude knows that just like all other emotions, happiness and joy are signs that they are operating in the present moment. Again, emoting then becomes an *opportunity* for reflection, sensing, and valuing something raw and real. The Green Attitude knows that happiness and joy visit us somewhat randomly and spontaneously, just like all the other emotions--so they don't try to hold onto or squeeze the life out of these moments. They maintain a humble approach and understanding, and see these positive feelings as a mindfulness barometer for where they're at in the journey of their life. It's an opportunity to reflect on the information that happiness and joy are communicating to them, and to enjoy knowing that they're on the right track.

The Red Attitude attaches itself to happiness and joy as if these feelings are things that can be taken away. When they've landed on the feelings of happiness and joy, they believe that they've succeeded; but if someone says or does something to interfere with this happiness and joy--they quickly become very upset with them. They do not realize that all feelings are just passing clouds in the sky, and that feelings are not constant nor are they facts! The Red Attitude believes that if they are not feeling happiness and joy, then *someone else* must not be doing something right. If a Red Attitude is experiencing happiness and joy and someone comes along who is sad and depressed, the Red Attitude will not allow any space for them. They will also shame them for showing up with these feelings as an affront to their own happy feelings.

Let's say for example that you're spending a nice evening with someone who primarily operates out of a Red Attitude, and you wish to bring up a serious topic with them for discussion. They may want to dismiss this topic you want to discuss and tell you to save it for a different time. They may say, "Let's just have a good time and not talk about this right now." For the Red Thinker, experiencing happiness is a *boastful* place to be, and you may hear them ask, "Why did you have to say that? I was so happy, and you just ruined it."

For the Blue Attitude, feeling happiness is often a result of someone else's happiness and joy. Blue Thinkers struggle internally to validate themselves, so they have to rely on how other people are feeling to gauge what they are allowed to feel. If someone in their personal life is struggling emotionally, and the Blue Attitude receives good news, they will feel guilty. They'll think it's *wrong* for them to be happy while their loved one is depressed. This type of thinking sounds like, "I can't be happy unless others are happy."

What about the Purple Thinker? What would they think about feeling happiness and joy? They may be unlikely to source this emotion since their thoughts won't allow it. This is a feeling that would be dismissed and seen as a mistake. "This can't be," they'll say. Or, "I never feel happiness. This must be a joke, there must be a hidden agenda somewhere. They may attach happiness to something that is unconventional like experiencing two weeks of non-stop rain and cloudiness-- knowing that it makes others so miserable.

Sadness

The Green Attitude allows for sadness when they feel sad, and they allow themselves to cry unapologetically. They express their sadness with the fullest level of vulnerability that it requires. They console and soothe themselves, as they would a small child. They talk openly about their sadness, but they won't expect others to make them feel better, because they accept that sadness is a natural feeling that we all have from time to time.

The Red Attitude will blame their sadness on someone else, and make others responsible for why they are feeling this way. The Red Attitude may feel shame for feeling sadness which they may turn into anger instead. The Red Attitude has difficulty sitting with vulnerable emotions on their own, and will seek the power in getting angry over sitting with sadness and depression. To the Red Thinker, feeling sadness is a weakness, as is crying and showing any vulnerable emotions. The Red Attitude may have the belief that no one wants to be around someone who is sad and depressed because no one cares or listens from this state; but when I'm angry and yelling I get the attention I need.

The Blue Attitude will apologize for crying in front of others, and will feel deep sorrow and pain in their heart when sadness overcomes them. They may hang onto this feeling of sadness beyond what is healthy, because it reminds them that "I Don't Matter," which seems to justify their existence. Some of us are attached to suffering and pain, so the familiarity of sadness can easily manifest into other types of suffering, such as physical pain. For the Blue Attitude, it seems like "No one cares about me if I'm happy," because when they're sad they get more attention from others. The sadness of always "losing" generates an attitude in their relationships with others, that despite how hard they try--they're constantly struggling to win.

The Purple Attitude is sad in a "who cares?" type of way. You wouldn't even know if they were truly sad. The Purple Thinker takes frustration and anger as proof for why humanity sucks, and that because we're forced to experience these feelings--we're all doomed. They see sadness and loneliness as a joke, and they make fun of themselves for having these "stupid" feelings. As will all emotions, the Purple Thinker struggles to fully connect with feelings of sadness.

Empathy

Empathy is a feeling that some have difficulty experiencing, and through our understanding of The 4 Mindsets, we can understand why. There are three levels of empathy: 1) cognitive, 2) emotional/affective, and 3) compassionate. If someone has fallen and scraped their knee, I can use my cognitive empathy to understand how that must have felt. Next I can actually *feel that pain* with emotional empathy, and then take action to help the person with their pain by offering compassion. Compassionate empathy would be treating the wound, or offering physical or emotional comfort. As I'm sure you can imagine, the Green Thinker possesses all of these levels of empathy within themselves. They are not only able to offer compassion to others, they are equally able to offer it to themselves.

The Red Thinker will struggle more with emotional empathy and compassion as they experience resistance in putting themselves in someone else's shoes. This will likely be a result of the "suck it up and get over it" programming. The Red Thinker struggles to relate with emotions that are not their own, and typically feel that someone is trying to manipulate them by showing empathy or compassion.

Because Non-Green Thinkers struggle with their own emotions and vulnerability, it's uncomfortable for them to be around others who are struggling. In the case of the Blue Thinker, their thoughts are "I feel good when other people feel good" and so their empathy can be over responsive and with a false sense of control. Empathy for Blue Thinkers can become toxic because their compassionate actions can go overboard which includes enabling unhealthy behaviors and making excuses for misbehavior in others.

The Purple Attitude struggles to understand the concept of compassion for others and themselves. Typically, they figure nothing can be done to help. If they were to come across someone who was in pain, they are unlikely to even notice. Since their thinking stems from a lose-lose objective, they've already shut themselves off from energetically picking up on the emotions of others, or if they were to notice, it would be viewed as a nuisance.

Feelings are Information

Everyone is their own energy source, emitting vibrational wavelengths sourced from *their own feelings*. Even when you can see that someone is in distress, and you ask them what's wrong––they may reply, "Nothing." Or if you ask someone if everything is okay, they usually reply, "I'm fine," even though the energy they're emanating says otherwise. This is why when your child sees their parents in distress they'll ask, "Are you okay? You look sad." Parents typically reply, "I'm fine, everything is okay, you don't need to worry." Through this response, we are actually invalidating their emotional intelligence. Even though it seems innocent, we're making them question their ability to empathize. Instead, we can be honest and tell them, "I'm struggling to figure something out right now, and it's making me feel a bit confused." We could even go so far as to ask them about a time they felt confused and help them in honing their own ability for self-compassion.

Many of us deny our true feelings, which is the same thing as denying our true selves. When we allow for the truth of our emotions to emerge, we can then be responsible for them. We can own them, honor them, and have compassion for them. Our feelings are not meant to be locked away or dismissed. When we do that, we end up *dismissing ourselves*. When we dismiss ourselves, and sweep our emotions under the rug , we sweep our true essence into the garbage.

Making the connection now between our thoughts and our feelings would show us that our thoughts are not technically painful, rather it's the feelings they evoke that can be. Conversely, it's not the uncomfortable feelings that are problematic, it's the way we think about them that is. Esther Hicks, channeler of Abraham Hicks often talks about *choosing the better-feeling thought.* Essentially, this is what we have control over. Feelings will arise, and consequently, so will thoughts. By embracing our feelings, we can link back to the circumstances upon which we are facing and use our feelings as a guide. Thus feelings are information and alert us to when we may have succumbed to insecure thoughts or behaviors that are not in our highest good. Our feelings also cue us to understanding when others behaviors are incongruent with the way we would like to be treated.

Being able to express our feelings serves to give others information about us. Therefore it's not only our own emotions that we need to be open to as guides, we also need to be open to listening and understanding the emotions from others as they hold important information in understanding what is important and meaningful in their own experiences.

Green Thinking is a way of learning how to *neutralize* your feelings, as well as the feelings of others. Green Thinking does not mean you will always be a positive, high-vibing person or expect others to be that way either. Let's not get pulled into the whole toxic positivity realm, that's not what this is about. It's about being honest about how you feel and learning how to hold a neutral viewpoint. Green Thinkers know that they may slip back into old attitudes from time to time, especially given the intense programming from the past, so they allow for and give themselves permission to experience that resistance from time to time without fully succumbing to an unconscious or insecure attitude.

A Green Attitude does not shame or judge themselves if this happens, instead they remember to just become cognizant of the shift. They know that the best thing to do when they're in an insecure way of thinking is to *simply catch it.* Just having the awareness that it's there is enough to return to a Green way of thinking. By catching yourself in Blue, Red, or Purple thinking is a very Green thing to do. The expectation isn't to change the thought or the feeling, rather to become aware of them and be a curious observer of what information may be hiding under the surface.

Having a Green Attitude doesn't mean you'll never experience negative emotions. It's true that the Green Thinker will experience a wide range of feelings--from happiness and joy, to anger, to frustration and shame. The difference is in what they *think* about these emotions that matters. This allows the Green Thinker to have a healthy relationship with their thoughts and feelings. When we acknowledge feelings of shame or guilt from a place of compassion and non-judgement, we put ourselves in a state of acceptance and offer ourselves an opportunity to learn about and connect with the discomfort, so that we can *move through it.* When we judge, deny, project, blame, or numb our feelings completely, this only contributes to further disconnection instead of deeper connections to yourself and others.

Saying Sorry For Feelings

Have you ever demanded someone apologize for hurting your feelings? Or maybe you've been the one profusely apologizing to someone in hopes of smoothing things over? When we operate from a Red Attitude we expect others to say sorry for the hurt feelings we perceive them to be the cause of. The Red Attitude thinks that if someone says, "I'm sorry for hurting your feelings," that this is going to make everything better. What they've actually done is they've mistakenly made their feelings your responsibility.

There may be times when we perceive disrespect from someone, and we think that we are entitled to respond to them in an equally disrespectful way. In that case, when we can catch ourselves thinking from this Red Attitude, it will immediately align ourselves with a Green Attitude. From there, we can apologize for our reaction and take responsibility for ourselves. It doesn't matter if our apology was received or not, what matters is that we counted ourselves by taking responsibility for our actions, and we counted the other person by acknowledging that this is not how they deserve to be treated, or spoken to.

The Blue Attitude would apologize for things that were not their fault. This reminds me of one of my first coaching clients who apologized to inanimate objects. By the end of our coaching her biggest win was overcoming her excessive need to apologize for everything when no apology was due. As a result she stopped taking responsibility for things that were not hers to take on and when she'd bump into things she'd laugh it off instead.

Offering apologies from a Non-Green, or insecure attitude will come across as either invalidating to ourselves or to others. Saying, "I'm sorry you feel that way," is invalidating and dismissive of the other person's experience. It implies that their feelings and perspective are somehow flawed or invalid. Instead we want to acknowledge their experience and demonstrate understanding and support. The Green approach would sound like "Thank you for letting me know how this made you feel. I can understand why you would feel that way, I'm sorry".

Being Responsible For Your Feelings and Holding Space For Others

Very few people can allow others to take responsibility for their own feelings, let alone validate and hold space for them. Let's say I come to you and complain, "I feel so tired and stressed. I've been so depressed lately. I just can't shake it."

You might say something like, "You need a night out. Let's go out for some drinks and forget about everything."

Others may respond differently such as, "Oh man, me too. I've been so tired and feeling so low, I can't understand why I've been feeling this way. I started talking to my therapist again and that really seems to be helping."

Another response might be, "Hey, you're doing so great though. You have a great job and a great family. Don't worry, things will get better."

Someone else may reply more proactively, "Thank you for being so honest with me. How long has this been going on? What have you done in the past that helped you feel better?"

Can you tell which color each of those statements are from? Let's look separately at each of these responses and see which one is the response that allows the other person to take responsibility for their feelings.

"You need a night out. Let's go out for some drinks and forget about everything."

This response tells the person what another assumes they need, and avoids having to engage in a conversation that involves vulnerability. This response also doesn't allow the individual to be validated or understood, and can be seen as dismissive of their emotional well-being. When we seek things outside of ourselves to feel better, this is only a distraction, a temporary fix to something that may require more long term care and attention. We're all guilty of seeking temporary relief from our pain, but the pain inevitably always comes back. Over time, this is when we can start to feel like something is wrong with us. The core issues need to be heard and addressed and then the solution needs to come from the person experiencing the pain. For many of us, just being heard can be so helpful instead of being told what we *should* do.

Oh man, me too. I've been so tired and feeling so low, I can't understand why I've been feeling this way. I started talking to my therapist again though, and that really seems to be helping.

This response takes the focus away from the other person's feelings and focuses on their own feelings and experiences instead. This can happen without us realizing what we're doing. We think that what helped us will help them. Maybe it will. However, when we start talking about ourselves, we're attempting to "fix them," or tell them what to do which has the effect of being invalidating.

Hey, you're doing so great though. You have a great job and a great family. Don't worry, things will get better.

I'm sure you're catching on by now, that this is another invalidating statement. It's true that sometimes we need to be reminded of the things that are going well for us in our lives, but by responding immediately in this fashion––we're dismissing the concerns that someone is trying to convey to us. We may feel uncomfortable hearing about someone's problems and not know how to respond, so we turn to the positive.

Thank you for being so honest with me. How long has this been going on? What have you done in the past that helped you feel better?

This statement is the most validating. There are questions to discover more and to encourage the person to seek solutions for themselves. Also you'll hear the words, "thank you" instead of, "sorry to hear that," or, "sorry you're feeling that way." Remember, we never need to be sorry for our feelings. Expressing gratitude toward someone who is being vulnerable with their feelings, will likely make them feel comfortable to share with you again. It's helpful to stop and question yourself in your responses to other's feelings by asking, "Is this response I'm giving them helpful for me? Or is this response helpful for them?" Opting for, "what's helpful to the situation right now," over, "what's helpful for me" will lead you more toward a win-win outcome.

9

Setting Boundaries

Setting Boundaries is the Highest Form of Self Care

At this point in the book, it's likely you're reevaluating your relationships, which is why understanding boundaries is important. Many people think that having healthy boundaries is a selfish way to be, and you can imagine what color attitude thinks that way. Others may view someone who sets boundaries as someone who has a lot of confidence or someone who is arrogant! By the end of this chapter on boundaries you will see how the act of setting boundaries is largely tied to self-respect and taking personal responsibility.

What do you think has to come first? Confidence or healthy boundaries? Healthy boundaries of course! When I first expressed a boundary with someone, or even with myself, I wasn't 100% confident, I questioned myself and I even ended up breaking my own boundaries. Developing an understanding of healthy boundaries is an essential component of personal growth, as it allows us to acknowledge and respect our needs. Through this process of trial and error, we become increasingly attuned to what takes us out of balance and what brings us closer to feeling aligned. Having this awareness allows us to recognise when our boundaries have been crossed. This is how our feelings come into play, remember, *feelings are information.* Without this awareness, we succumb to disempowerment as we struggle to establish a sense of alignment with what our values and personal preferences are. With that, our confidence suffers, and we may miss or dismiss the signs of violation or disrespect, thus missing the opportunity to assert boundaries.

Ultimately, setting boundaries is the path toward self-empowerment. As you set boundaries, even with yourself, you gain confidence in your abilities to set boundaries with others. The most important goal of healthy boundaries is to foster and promote healthy relationships. Having healthy boundaries is a sign of good self-esteem and generally indicates that we are secure in our relationships with others. You are free to set boundaries with everything and everyone you like--but first and foremost--you need to set the majority of your boundaries within yourself.

How Do I Set Boundaries With Myself?

Most of the people that have come to work with me either don't know what their needs are, don't know how to communicate them, or they don't feel worthy of them. So I ask them, "What needs do you take care of for others?"

Here are some of the responses:

- Money
- Meals and food
- Talking about their problems and giving advice
- Driving
- Doing nice things to show love
- Cleaning up
- Giving praise and validation
- Checking in
- Spending quality time together

The things we do for others, we also need to do for ourselves. If you are a person who is constantly doing *all of this* for others *all the time,* it's unlikely that you give yourself the same attention.

Turning these things into personal boundaries for ourselves would sound like this:

- I have a budget and boundaries when it comes to how I spend my money.
- I make sure that I nourish myself and get to bed on time.
- I give myself compassion and take my problems seriously.
- I tend to the obligations and appointments that I have for myself first.
- I show myself love and treat myself to the simple pleasures of life.
- I tend to my home with care and ensure that it's a space that I feel comfortable in.
- I speak to myself kindly and give myself credit for my accomplishments.
- I check in with myself and ask how I'm feeling.

- I ask myself what I need when I'm feeling anxious, sad, or upset.
- I spend time alone or with others, doing the things that bring me joy.

Setting boundaries is how we teach other people how to treat us. This is why we have to start establishing and honoring personal boundaries within ourselves first. In this way, we become role models to others on how to set healthy boundaries for themselves. We cannot expect someone to treat us with respect, show compassion, or speak kindly––if we don't already do this for ourselves.

Boundaries are not about controlling others, they're about taking responsibility for ourselves. When we fall into a pattern of being responsible for outside cues and making outside cues responsible for our feelings and behaviors, either we're trying to control things we have no control over, or we're unconsciously *allowing* ourselves to be controlled. Without healthy boundaries, other people can be in control, resulting in a power imbalance and powerlessness. When all of our actions are driven by outside cues, we no longer act from our inner authority and may even lose our sense of identity. Over time this is how people end up *losing themselves*. They no longer know what makes them happy or what they're passionate about. They stop pursuing their own goals, because they've fallen into the trap of making other people happy.

What if you were never able to establish your own identity? What if you've always allowed others to define who you are, instead of allowing yourself to discover your self-worth intrinsically? This is very common for people raised in codependent families, or with what we call "helicopter parents." Without a real sense of self outside of feeling responsible for others, how is it possible for someone to validate and take responsibility for their own interests and wellbeing? They can't. They'll have a hard time saying, "No" with the belief that boundaries are selfish and mean.

Without boundaries we bleed into the identity of others. Saying things like, "Whatever you want." Or, "If you're happy, then I'm happy." Or, "I'm easy, I'll do anything." Or, "Whatever is best for you" is normal to say once in awhile, it's part of being flexible--but if you find yourself responding like this all the time, and lacking a definitive stance or ability to make a decision for yourself based on your own desires, then you're not affording yourself the opportunity to express your own individuality.

Get In The Driver's Seat of Your Life

Boundaries are put into place so that we have a sense of safety in the world. Think of your boundaries like a car. Your boundaries are like the seat belt and the brakes of your car. The seat belt holds you back from interfering in other people's spaces, giving unsolicited advice, or telling people what to do. The brakes allow you to stop when you have taken on too much, and to slow down when the balance is about to tip. It's also helpful to use those turn signals to let people know the direction you are heading beforehand.

People will appreciate knowing your intentions ahead of time so that nothing comes as a surprise. Still, you may notice that some people will get into "your car" and tell you how you *should* be driving it. The *backseat driver* lacks healthy boundaries of their own and likes to be in control. We need to let people know that this may not be the way in which they would drive their car--but this is what *works for you*.

What if your car breaks down on the side of the road? This can happen if we haven't been diligent with proper car maintenance. Maybe we ran out of gas, or ignored those squeaky brakes. Sometimes these things can be easily fixed, like filling up your tank, but you might not know how to fix the brakes and may need to seek professional help. We may sneer at how much it costs us to make these repairs, but the alternative is driving around in an unsafe vehicle, or not being able to drive anymore at all. We pay the cost to keep our car safe to drive, and it's no different than paying a therapist or a coach to get us back into the driver's seat of our lives, so that we can feel safe to continue traveling on our path. The key to all of this? Life's balance is found in boundaries.

Balance is Found In Boundaries

Take care to notice when you may have gone out of alignment with your true self by taking things personally, not getting enough rest, being harsh and critical with yourself, permitting disrespectful behavior, and pushing yourself past your limits. An inside cue that will often let us know when we've done this is the feeling of anxiety. I notice that this feeling of anxiety will arise whenever I've compromised myself or when I haven't been considerate of other people's needs.

Boundaries serve as a framework that allows you to establish a sense of equilibrium in various aspects of your life by prioritizing your needs, protecting your energy, fostering healthy relationships, managing your time and commitments, and enhancing your ability to practice self-care. Since everything is an energy, when I set healthy boundaries for myself, I am letting myself know that I matter and others matter too! When I take care of my energy, then I have it to share with others.

Boundaries can be set and defined in terms of how we use our time, how we honor our physical self, emotional and mental wellbeing, financial health, spiritual well being, and sexual preferences. All of these contribute to our energetic input and output. If all we are doing is exerting ourselves to accommodate other people's wants and needs, then our energy will be depleted. Let's take a closer look at some of these often overlooked boundaries that we need to be responsible for within ourselves.

Emotional Boundaries

I am responsible for my boundaries, however,

I am *not* responsible for how you respond to them.

Establishing healthy emotional boundaries is probably the hardest, yet most important for our emotional wellbeing. Having healthy emotional boundaries means that you don't take responsibility for other people's feelings, and you don't expect others to be responsible for yours. For those who consider themselves to be empathic and highly sensitive, it's easy to take on other people's feelings as if they were your own. To a certain degree, having empathy and compassion for others is a gift and one that is a benefit in our relationships at work and with family and friends. At the same time, it can also be to our own detriment and become toxic, because feeling responsible for other people's emotions isn't a healthy way to be.

A common issue for empathic people when communicating their preferences involves responding to the emotional reactions they get from other people. Because of their inability to understand how emotional boundaries work, they might think that setting any boundary with someone, means that this will be a *lose* for them. If I get asked to cat-sit for my friend again, but their cat makes my allergies go off the charts, and I can't sleep very well, as a result I have to say 'no'. They may get upset with me and say, "well this was never a problem before." And I'm thinking, that's because I never said anything before and instead I just *sucked it up*. But I don't want to do that to myself again, so I must let them know my situation. I can let them know that although I was happy to help before, they won't be able to expect this from me anymore. I don't even need to apologize for this. Instead I can thank them for considering me, and wish them well in finding a new cat-sitter.

Remember the Green Attitude aims to not leave anyone

any worse off then where we found them. In this case, the person still needs to find someone to watch their cat while they're away. We haven't done anything to make their needs any different. And it's ok if they're disappointed, that's understandable. So we hold an emotional boundary that lets them know we understand their disappointment, and we also understand that we are not responsible for their disappointment. We could give a different friend the same reply and they respond with disappointment, but they also respond with understanding, and empathy and may offer us condolences instead.

It's common to feel some level of guilt when we're unable to fulfill someone else's request. This feeling of guilt lets us know that we care, and that we wish we could help. Carrying it around as if we've done something wrong however is unhealthy. For people who take on the emotions of others and feel responsible for them, the majority of their lives will be plagued by this unhealthy guilt. If this is something you've been trying to resolve, establishing emotional boundaries is crucial. A key reminder that we need to tell ourselves is, "They're an outside cue and I am not responsible for outside cues. I cannot change them, and I am not in control of them. I am only responsible for how I choose to respond to them."

If your mother complains that she's lonely because you don't visit her enough, this is her attempting to make you responsible for her feelings of loneliness. If you caved and started to visit her more often, you'd be confirming that you are responsible for her feelings. When we teach people that we are responsible for their feelings, they'll continue to expect emotional energy from us, which can be detrimental in the long-term.

Instead, you can set a boundary with your mom by letting her know that you care and acknowledge her feelings of loneliness and let her know that you will visit when you're available to do so. Internally remind yourself that it is her responsibility to make friends and take responsibility for her isolation and loneliness. Remind yourself that you are not the cause nor are you the solution to her feelings of loneliness.

Could she be operating from a Red Attitude? Ask yourself questions about the situation to make sure your thoughts are coming from a Green Attitude before you set this emotional boundary for yourself. Did you catch how I said, *for yourself*, instead of *for your mother*? This is how we exemplify that boundaries are about what *we will do*, instead of how we want others to be.

Setting emotional boundaries not only involves drawing the line between your emotions and someone else's, it also means that you have the emotional maturity to take responsibility for your own feelings. Since we cannot rely on others to know what is best for us, we learn how we want to be treated through how others are already treating us. Just as setting boundaries teaches others how we want to be treated, when we are operating from a Green Attitude, we are open to learning about ourselves. When we've had an experience that highlights the need for a boundary, a Green Attitude can unbiasedly evaluate the experience instead of blaming others, and take ownership for itself.

Which Color Attitude Struggles With Emotional Boundaries?

The Blue Attitude is most susceptible to taking on the emotions of others, and rely on the other person to feel better so they can feel better. There is no distinction between their emotions and someone else's emotions, just that they are responsible to make the other person feel good. If a friend told a Blue Thinker that they felt hopeless after losing their job, the Blue Thinker might later tell *another friend* that they were feeling helpless because *their friend* just lost their job. This is how the Blue Attitude takes on other people's problems as if they were their own. For the Blue Attitude, there is no distinction between what are my problems to resolve and what problems belong to others to resolve.

The Red Attitude will also have difficulty with emotional

boundaries in a much different way because they think their feelings *are* the responsibility of others. They also have the belief that outside cues are the cause of their emotions. When the Red Attitude tells someone they lost their job and expresses anger with their colleagues for "throwing them under the bus"––they will expect whoever is listening to take action. They don't like it when you just "hold space" for them. Instead, they want you to help them sue the company, find a new job, or hire them to work for you. If you're not on their side, then you're against them. As you can tell, this is why the Red Attitude enjoys the company of the Blue Attitude so much.

The Blue Attitude will place an unnecessary expectation on themselves to solve other people's problems, so that they can prove their worth. When you have two people struggling with boundaries in a relationship, there will be many extreme ups and downs. The Blue Attitude will never be able to solve the problems of a Red Attitude, and the Red Attitude will always feel like others are to blame. In an insecure relationship, people will forego having boundaries just to be accepted. When we shift into a Green way of thinking, it doesn't matter if someone doesn't understand our feelings, and can't help us with our problems, what matters first and foremost is that we do!

Mental Boundaries

Mental boundaries, or intellectual boundaries, are what keep us out of useless debates, being guilt tripped, engaging in pointless arguments, and gossiping. Many people who follow my social media accounts ask how to set boundaries with their family. These are typically the family members we either learned, or didn't learn, boundaries from in the first place. If healthy boundaries were not modeled for you in your family, then it's likely your family still has unhealthy boundaries. When you engage with a family member who holds a Red Attitude regarding the importance of tending to our needs, and you approach them with your Green Attitude, it is unlikely that they will immediately or possibly ever respond favorably.

No one can respond positively to your boundaries unless they are open to operating from the Green Mindset. Attempting to express your needs or different perspectives with a Red Attitude is likely to result in fighting, constant defending of oneself, and wasted emotional energy. It's important to recognize the mindset that other people are coming from, and take that into consideration when we establish mental boundaries. When we understand and accept that someone's anger stems from the way they are thinking then it's easier to not take things personally and instead shut down those conversations that are unproductive. By setting mental boundaries for ourselves, we effectively manage our mental energy and save ourselves from mental exhaustion.

It is worth acknowledging that some traditional values or expectations within certain cultures or religions may prioritize obedience, or self-sacrifice, which can potentially pose challenges to the practice of healthy boundaries. In these cases, the ability to count yourself in a Green way can be challenging and discouraged. In this case, all you can do is remind yourself what you do have control over, which is the way you treat yourself.

Our family members may not be mentally or intellectually capable of understanding that boundaries can come from a healthy and loving place. Unfortunately, the only consequence to developing an ever-growing Green Attitude, is that we may lose people from our lives who cannot for whatever reason connect to the Green Attitude. We cannot tell other people, including our family, how to think, or convince them of a belief or a new way of being. We must take into consideration their own personal experiences and perceptions, and once again, remind ourselves that they are an outside cue, and we can't change outside cues. We can only change how we choose to respond to them. You have to ask yourself though, do you feel healthier and freer when not intertwined with a Red, Blue, or Purple Attitude? The answer is most likely, yes.

Boundaries From a Different Perspective

Let's look at healthy boundaries from the perspective of being a dog owner. Part of being a responsible pet owner means that you have to take your dog out for plenty of walks. If you were to allow the dog to take the lead, and instead of walking the dog, the dog was walking you! You've now given the responsibility of walking your dog over to your dog! Cesar Milan, known as the *Dog Whisperer,* teaches dog owners how to be the *leader of the pack* by letting their dog know that they are in charge.

We can't assume that a dog automatically knows what is acceptable behavior, it doesn't. We have to teach them, and this can mean doing the same thing over and over, even hundreds of times, before they fully learn what is expected of them. This is not to say that I'm comparing the people in our lives to dogs, but dogs learn very much in the same way that humans do. With a dog in charge, you'll be feeling exhausted while constantly explaining their poor behavior and apologizing every time they bark, jump up, or destroy your guests shoes. It is vital that they are shown and taught what is expected of them, because if they aren't, they'll run amok.

Some of us find that it's easier to let other people, or dogs, have their way, instead of investing time and energy into establishing healthy boundaries and doing the work. They hope that everyone else will just have some "common sense" and automatically adjust to suit their needs. However, when we allow the insecure version of ourselves to be in charge, we allow everyone else to have power over us. Just like the dog that thinks it's in charge of us, so will the people we spend time with.

I have a friend who paid $3500 for a dog trainer to teach her how to establish proper ground work and respect between her and her dog. She said it was worth every penny. Her dog doesn't jump up, doesn't bark unnecessarily, and walks alongside instead of in front of her. The relationship between her and her dog is one of mutual respect. It's a win-win.

Her dog doesn't feel anxious and unsure about its behavior. Instead it knows exactly what is expected of him, which allows the dog to enjoy a safe and secure relationship with its owner.

When we start asserting boundaries, or while in the process of training a dog, our energy may come across as nervous or anxious, which can result in others feeling unsure as to whether or not they can trust if what we're asking for is really necessary. This is the time when we'll experience push back as others try to exert control over us. If we back down and dismiss our own needs, we teach them that our needs don't matter. Our confidence is crushed again and again. Don't give up! With time and consistent practice, our confidence grows. Just like training a dog, when we invest the time into teaching them acceptable behavior we become very confident dog owners.

By the way, dogs are much easier to train than humans and we need to know the difference between someone who is willing to learn, versus someone who isn't. As you continue to practice setting boundaries, your energy will relax, and you will get less and less push back from others. People will start to respect you more and you will come to respect that it's also ok if people don't respect your boundaries. They don't have to. But *you* do!

Boundaries Build Bridges Not Walls

If you've been a Blue Thinker who hasn't set boundaries, and one day you decide that you've had enough and that you're not going to allow people to take advantage of you anymore--you may find yourself trying to set boundaries now from a Red Attitude. You might think that this is the attitude that makes boundaries and sticks with them. Saying 'no' to everyone, and being very rigid with your boundaries, might be empowering at first, but over time it will not be effective in building healthy relationships. Boundaries set from a Red Attitude are what build walls, not bridges. However, there is one small caveat to this: putting up a wall with a toxic person may be necessary at some point in our lives.

Overall, boundaries are most effective when done with a Green Attitude. Healthy boundaries create healthy relationships. A common error is making the assumption that people *should* know what we want, or that people *should* just automatically know how to treat us. This mindset of making assumptions, will land us in a lose-lose outcome. Have you heard the saying when you assume, you make an ass out of you and me? You'll notice this saying within the word *ass-u-me.* We can't leave our needs to other people to figure out. And we also need to stop *shoulding* on people. Either people want to know what our needs are and will seek to understand them, or they won't. Most of the time we don't even know what our own needs are!

When we take the time to understand what our needs and wants are, then we can start to honor them in ourselves and *effectively* communicate them to others. This is how we build bridges to the people that matter most to us, and allows them to connect with us in a way that provides the ultimate level of mutual respect and understanding.

Here are some examples of things we say that unknowingly build walls:

"You should be more considerate and thoughtful"

What color attitude might be thinking in this way? This statement creates a wall because it sends a message to the other person that they are not being thoughtful or considerate. What is usually the underlying reason why someone feels that another isn't considering them? Often it's because they don't feel heard or understood.

When communicated from a Green Attitude:

"I feel misunderstood when you make comments like that. I need to know that I'm being heard and understood by you when I'm expressing my feelings so we can communicate better."

In this example, the individual counts themselves by expressing their needs. This isn't just a need they have for this one person—–this is a need they have for all people in their life. If their reaction is to get defensive and shift into blame, then they may be unwilling to meet them on the bridge they're trying to create. Some individuals may feel intimidated when others use assertive communication which results in their resistance to communicate in the same way.

"You're always late. I need you to be on time."

Telling someone what to do based on undesirable behavior will always lead to building walls. Remember, we cannot control how others act and we are only responsible for our own behavior. A better boundary would sound something like:

"If you're going to be more than five minutes late, I'll have to leave without you. I'll just meet you there."

A bridge was created to allow the other person to continue to operate in whatever behavior they choose. The individual has chosen to let go of the need to control and allow others to make their own decisions. Someone who is late all the time is likely experiencing other underlying factors. Just telling them to be on time isn't going to fix any of that, and will likely just exacerbate it.

"Don't talk to me like that, it's rude and disrespectful and I won't have it!"

This is a controlling demand that will immediately put up a wall. Whenever we tell someone how we *don't* want them to be, we usually end up getting more of that unwanted behavior. Instead, it's helpful to tell the other person what the desired behavior is. This may come out as a request such as:

"Please speak to me in a calm voice." Or, "I feel disrespected when you yell at me and tell me those things.

I need you to speak to me in a calm voice so we can both be understood and communicate better"

This sets the tone for how you want to be treated, instead of how you don't want to be treated. We build a bridge to allow the communication to continue under certain expectations. If they are unable to meet those requests, then we let them know that we can't speak to them until they're able to do so.. This puts up a temporary wall, however, the bridge is still open for them to connect with when they're ready.

I've used a little formula in the last and first example that you may have noticed. This formula is a great tool to use when you want to aim to communicate effectively and assertively. It goes like this:

I feel ______________________________
When you ______________________________
I need ______________________________
So we can ______________________________

Using this formula requires you to stop and think first about the feeling you are experiencing from this situation. Take care not to say "I feel *that*..., because by adding the word "that" to your feelings, you are forming an opinion instead of connecting to your feelings. Then you let the person know what it is they are doing that is cueing this feeling for you, in as few words as possible, and without judgment. Remember to own your feelings instead of making the outside cue responsible for them.

Then we formulate the "I need" statement, which is essentially where the boundary shows up. And finally the last sentence which is aiming for a win-win outcome. Both of the examples I used indicated, "so we can communicate better" and essentially, that is the goal with setting boundaries. Once they understand what it is you need and how it would benefit them too, it's then up to them to decide if they will comply or not. And if not, then we have to follow through on the consequences which could be taking a time out, leaving the conversation, or depending on how serious it is, making the decision to change the terms of the relationship.

Here are a few other examples of how we may unknowingly be creating walls by not having healthy boundaries:

"I prefer that my wife includes me when she goes out with her friends. She knows how jealous I can get in these situations, so she usually just ends up staying home with me instead."

The wall in this case is between the wife and her friends. This is an example of an unhealthy *emotional boundary* as the husband is making his wife responsible for his feelings of jealousy. In this example, the husband needs to set a boundary *with himself*. He needs to acknowledge his feelings of jealousy as *information*. How can he create a bridge instead of this wall? My suggestion would be that he take responsibility for his insecurities instead of making his wife responsible for it. Working through this emotion will allow a bridge to form as well as a connection back to himself, which is currently broken.

One other comment I would make is that the husband may have a legitimate cause for his jealousy. Perhaps his wife cheated on him in the past, and he decided to stay in the relationship under these terms. Or this feeling could stem from a memory of his past when he was betrayed. Rebuilding trust can be a difficult process in any relationship, and in this case both of them will need to work on building a more secure bridge back to each other, since it appears that this bridge seems to be under construction.

"The people I work with are useless, so I'm always late to meetings because I spend all of my time telling them how to do their jobs."

The wall here is created by seeing coworkers as useless. There is no bridge which would allow for mistakes or failures and have empathy for the learning process. Again, a boundary needs to be made within themselves, to allow the bridge for their colleagues to make mistakes and take initiative on their own. The individual in this example feels responsible for the work of their colleagues, and it's clearly taking a negative toll on their own reputation as an employee by showing up late to meetings. I'd say the color at play here is a Red Attitude.

"My mother would never forgive me if I moved out of state, even though I've been offered several high paying jobs that I'm very passionate about."

In this example, the person is creating a wall within themselves. The mother may have contributed to this wall by placing demands on them to always be there for her, and as a result, has left them with a fear of rejection, or abandonment. As we know, setting boundaries with family members is the most difficult. However, this person is sacrificing their own passions for the mother's needs. This individual assumes that their mother would never forgive them, and although their mother would genuinely miss them, this is a great opportunity for both of them to develop a secure level of interdependence. They could both make compromises to call and visit, while still pursuing their own goals and reaching success, instead of feeling stifled. One other factor to consider is that this person may have a fear of success or a fear of failure. If they just play things safe and stay on familiar territory, they won't have to face the, "Am I good enough for this job?" question. Or, "What if I'm actually not as good as they think I am?" question. Imposter syndrome can underlie some of the Blue, self-sabotaging behaviors.

"My best friend gets really angry with me when I don't include her in my plans, so I have to make sure that I always remember to invite her."

It sounds like this friend has an insecurity that may stem from a Red Attitude. Whether the individual placed this expectation on themselves, or it was placed on them by the friend, this is an unreasonable expectation to put on oneself, and it creates a wall through tension and emotional instability.

A personal boundary would need to be established within that says, "It's okay to not include my best friend in everything that I do, and it's healthy to have plans on my own or with others from time to time. I can still be a good friend without having to be responsible for her feelings of jealousy and anger."

We build bridges by establishing healthy boundaries that make it safe for others to spend time with us. It's helpful to let them know that we value them as a friend and enjoy spending time with them. However, if they continue to make such demands and are unable to respect the terms that have been established, then we may have to erect a wall to prevent toxic connections any further. This is how we count ourselves, while we also count the other person by encouraging them to move into a more Green approach. We may have to establish a rigid boundary in this case for protection and as a consequence to their inability to respect boundaries. This might result in the end of a friendship or less time spent together.

The Mindset Where Boundaries are Made

Of course we do not lose sight of *The 4 Mindsets* as they play the most important role in setting boundaries. As we know our thoughts are what dictate our behavior, and when we set boundaries from an insecure place, they will not end in a win-win outcome. The win-win outcome is how we build the bridge and connection to forming meaningful, healthy relationships.

Let's consider the scenario of a coworker consistently interrupting and talking over not only you, but also others during a team meeting. If you approached this scenario from a Red Attitude, you may interrupt this person in the meeting and speak to them in a way that is equally disrespectful just to get your point across. At first it may feel like a win for you because you feel relieved and satisfied to finally say something to them, but ultimately it's a loss for them because they got called out in front of everyone and may be left feeling a sense of shame about their behavior. They may then respond to you in a Red Attitude and this could wind up headed for a lose-lose outcome and essentially building a wall.

The cause behind someone interrupting is unknown to us, and we may have already formed assumptions and judgements about why they do this, but it also could be an innocent behavior. Many times, individuals who face challenges with executive functioning, tend to interrupt others not out of disrespect, but driven by a sincere eagerness to actively contribute to the conversation.

A Blue Attitude setting a boundary in this area, would also be unsuccessful since their communication would come across too passive and wishy-washy. They end up telling the person, "It's ok, I don't mind, but sometimes you cut me off when I'm talking, and it just bothers me, but don't worry, it's not a big deal, I just wanted to let you know and it can be a bit frustrating for me, and I think other people might be feeling the same way too." Now I know this doesn't *sound* too bad, and is one of the reasons why many of us with a Blue Attitude will convince themselves that they are in the Green with their thinking.

The Blue Attitude in this example does well to express their feelings, but in doing so, they also invalidate themselves. This may result in the individual hearing this to think it's still ok to interrupt, because it's not a big deal anyway. There's also a mention of "other people" feeling the same way, which we want to avoid speaking on behalf of others.

It's unlikely that someone with a Blue Attitude will set boundaries to begin with and when these insecure attitudes want to make a shift toward counting themselves, there will be a tendency for them to adopt a Red Attitude instead of Green. This is especially true when the Blue Attitude is up against someone whom they perceive to be a Red Attitude. It's much easier to get mad and say, "That's it, I've had enough of this and I'm going to stand up for myself," than to consider the needs of someone who is operating from a Red Attitude How can we possibly give consideration to someone who isn't giving us the same in return?

No other mindset can consider the diversity of other people like the Green Attitude can. A Green Attitude would wait until after the meeting and would have this conversation in private as they consider and count the needs of the other person. They also count the other members of the team to communicate one on one, instead of potentially bringing everyone into this scenario. The Green Thinker may say something like, "I noticed that you're really involved in the discussions in our team meetings which is great as you have so many helpful ideas to offer. I have been feeling frustrated in these meetings when you interrupt me when I'm speaking. I need to be able to express my views and ideas, and hear other people talking one at a time so we can maintain a more respectful communication dynamic during meetings."

Internal Boundaries and External Boundaries

Just like inside cues and outside cues, which are the ones we have control over? When we are always focused on setting boundaries with outside cues and other people we grow frustrated and upset because they're not doing what we want them to.

What we tend to overlook are the boundaries within ourselves, the ones that *we do* have control over. This is of course much more difficult because taking responsibility for ourselves requires more effort than handing it over to others to do for us. Having a level of personal responsibility will take you much further than being responsible for the behavior changes in others.

It's easier for us to blame outside cues on why we're feeling frustrated than actually managing that emotion within ourselves first. Remember the chapter on taking 100% responsibility, this is where we apply this to boundary setting. It's always advisable to look at the ways in which we are blaming others for our displeasure before we decide to talk to them about it.

American motivational author, Louise Hay has a quote that I find myself returning to often which says, "I do not fix problems, I fix my thinking and then problems fix themselves." This is a good reminder that our perceptions from insecure thoughts will cause insecure reactions. While thoughts from the Green Attitude will result in the shifts necessary to see how certain problems are not really problems at all, rather just a problem with the way we were thinking about them. The more time you spend operating from a Green Attitude, the less time you spend reacting to outside cues.

From Boundaries to Being

One day you won't need boundaries anymore. Ha! How is that possible? Well, because eventually you're just going to just BE! What are you going to be? You're going to be your authentic self.

Without boundaries, you've been fulfilling everyone else's needs and not your own. When you have boundaries in place, you show yourself respect and honor your authentic self. Once your boundaries are clearly established, you are free to move into a state of acceptance, courage, love, willingness, and gratitude. All of which is who you really are!

By embracing a Green Attitude more and more, you can transcend the confines of societal expectations, fears, and self-imposed limitations. As a result, you will authentically operate from a place of genuine truth, instead of worrying about having to set boundaries with everyone out of a place of insecurity and fear. Now you can just be.

Being your true self means you are an autonomous being, which is one that leads from their truth and core self. I know that whenever I am acting from a Green way of thinking, that I am also acting in good faith. This gives me peace of mind to know that even when others don't respond favorably to my boundaries, I don't take it personally. Once you can let go of taking these things personally, you'll realize that you are the only one in charge of you, which results in a splendid sense of liberation.

Along this journey you've learned not only how to set boundaries, you've also learned to listen to the quiet voice within, which has helped you understand your unique strengths while also accepting your weaknesses so you can make choices that resonate with your core values. Instead of experiencing the imbalance of give-and-take, we engage in a balanced energy exchange. Instead of needing love or giving love, we share love. Instead of giving time or taking time, we share time with others. Instead of giving compassion or receiving compassion, we share compassion.

When we are in tune with our own energy, we know that we can always meet our own needs. We know when our sharing with others is not reciprocated, we can savor it and save it, instead of spending it frivolously on those who don't have our best interest at heart. We build bridges to connect and stay open and accessible to others, knowing that we can put the *Do Not Enter* sign up on a bridge whenever we need to.

10

The Mindful Green Attitude

Mindfulness is kindfulness.
Mindfulness is compassion.
Mindfulness is listening without fixing.

Mindfulness is Everything

You've probably heard the saying, "Mindset is everything." I'd say more so that *mindfulness* is everything. Within the practice of being mindful, we give ourselves the opportunity to increase our level of conscious awareness. Mindfulness has us notice the beliefs that are limiting our ability to engage in meaningful relationships, which then cues us to the process of changing our mindset. Mindfulness is the ability to be in the present moment on purpose, and without judgment. The "without judgment" is the biggest challenge we face when practicing mindfulness. The ability to be non-judgemental toward ourselves--especially when we have uncomfortable or undesirable thoughts and feelings is what allows us to enter into a Green Attitude. This is why I place the practice of mindfulness above mindset work, because in order to change your thoughts, you have to have an awareness of them. It's ok to have judgment so long as we catch it and don't judge our judging! Once we become increasingly more attuned to our thoughts and how they make us feel, we'll be able to recognize judgemental thoughts and judgemental responses more easily, allowing this conditioned and automatic response to slowly lessen over time. We catch it, give ourselves credit for catching it, and then change our perspective.

I've learned over the years that "neurons that fire together, wire together" and that we can always form new neural pathways by training our brains through deliberate and focused attention. Mindset changes require an acceptance of those periods of instability and as well as a solid belief that you can change. We can become very attached to our thoughts and accept them as facts, which over time leaves us in a fixed, or stagnant mindset, which leaves us thinking that we're unable to change.

It's common for us to turn away from experiences that are hurtful. Mindfulness asks us to *turn into* these experiences. You can always bring your thoughts and feelings into a neutral position. By doing so, you allow yourself to become a better communicator and increase your ability to deal with stressful situations. When you notice a feeling or a thought that is causing distress, instead of turning away from it, turn inward with compassion and acceptance. Within the practice of mindful awareness, acceptance enters, and once in a state of acceptance, you'll find choices instead of limitations. Choosing to be in the present moment without judgment takes practice, and with practice you learn that you always have the ability to recenter and recalibrate yourself back to the here and now.

Finding The Middle Path: Mindful Being vs. Mindless Doing

Finding the middle path is a way to remove yourself from "all or nothing" thinking. Some of us are attached to dualistic words like "good and bad," "right and wrong," or "love and hate." We may paint everyone with the same brush, making statements like, "Nobody loves me." Or, "Everyone is a jerk." When I walk the middle path, I challenge myself to understand how right and wrong can exist *at the same time*. If I seek to change the world, I remind myself that the only thing I can change is myself--because by changing myself, I'm *indirectly* changing the world and how I see it.

Dr. Marsha Linehan developed the Dialectical Behavioural Theory (DBT) in 1980 as a method to work with people who are extremely sensitive to rejection and invalidation. Much of what I present to you with The 4 Mindsets is based on the CBT model which is very effective in teaching us how to change our thoughts, feelings and behaviors. The DBT approach teaches us how to walk the middle path between change and acceptance. Dialectics means accepting that two things can be possible at the same time, such as the fact that life can be challenging, and it's also rewarding.

In a nutshell, DBT focuses on emotional regulation, mindfulness and acceptance to solve problems and to make changes to our behavior. When I notice that I'm in a state of resistance, the practice of mindfulness allows me to notice it, which puts me into a state of *acceptance of my resistance*. In this way, I understand how I can be both in a state of resistance, and a state of acceptance of my resistance, at the same time. It's often the ego that likes to choose extremes. The ego likes to exist in the past or the future, it doesn't like to slow down and be in the present moment. The ego is judging and unforgiving. The mindful Green approach encourages us to focus on solving problems in the moment, without bringing up the past, or worrying about the future.

Consider this example: The ego stays attached to a thought that one's mother doesn't care about them, because she never told them that she loved them. From this, the ego would sink into despair and sadness or wallow in hate and disappointment. Mindfulness and a mindful Green Attitude would allow for a detachment from this thought, and create a distance from self-judgment. The person could then freely ask themselves, "Is this a fact, or is this a belief?" There may be a very strong feeling that says it's a fact, even though it isn't. Finding the truth in the present moment brings a person to the conclusion that negative beliefs no longer serve them. A new belief, that one's mother does care about them even if she doesn't say the words, "I love you," can easily replace an old one. This new belief would allow for both things to be true at the same time and in this case it would be, "my mother loves me even though she doesn't say it."

When we take care to find the middle path, an understanding of our mother's experience is considered, and instead of concluding that she doesn't care--we can move into a state of compassion. Mindfulness encourages us to be more curious about our thoughts, explore different ways of thinking, and consider different perspectives. Judgemental thoughts will naturally arise, so the key is to notice the judgment in the present moment, and then remind ourselves again not to judge our judging.

Through this process, we can achieve a state of neutrality that in no way implies indifference or even full detachment.

Instead, it allows us to respond in a balanced and open-hearted way, resulting in feelings of contentment and acceptance, instead of the hurt or anger that would have been there before. Now that we're thinking differently, we can act differently. We may choose to engage with our mother more frequently from this new perspective, as opposed to being avoidant with her. Or we may choose to have limited interactions with her, but from a compassionate space.

When we are consciously aware of how our *doing* is impacting our *being*, we move into alignment with our true selves. A mindless *doing* goes about life operating from an insecure and unaware attitude. A mindful *being* not only considers how their actions impact others, but also how their actions impact themselves. Staying on the middle path becomes the way to stay in alignment with all that is possible. From here, we can allow ourselves to have thoughts that are incongruent, while simultaneously recognizing the dichotomy that exists.

The Tao Te Ching has taught me how to see the middle path when rigid Red or Blue thoughts enter. Within the Tao, which literally means "the way" you'll find mindful passages to help illustrate the dialectics in finding the middle path. Here is Stephen Mitchell's interpretation of Lao Tzu's words, and how the two sides are captured:

She is good to people who are good.
She is also good to people who aren't good.
This is true goodness.
She trusts people who are trustworthy.
She also trusts people who aren't trustworthy.
This is true trust.[10]

If you are good to people who are good, while you're also good to those who are not good, this reflects the ultimate good that lives within you--regardless of how others are behaving, because of course you don't have control over that. You can trust in yourself to act responsibly, even when others lack the ability to do so. You can operate from a Green

Attitude and show goodness to all by considering both sides, without the need to enter into an 'all or nothing', or fight-or-flight response. You can respond from a free-flow-fun place of safety and security instead, because you are not threatened by the behaviors of others. You can also trust yourself to respond in a way that considers and respects the best interest of everyone involved.

How can you trust someone that is trustworthy and trust someone who is untrustworthy? The Green Attitude would say that they afford everyone an equal opportunity. If someone originally appeared untrustworthy, that doesn't mean that they will forever be someone that can't be trusted. The Tao also says, "If you don't trust the people, you make them untrustworthy." Or, "When a leader trusts no one, no one trusts him." Therefore trust becomes a reflection of what you are projecting from within. The practice of mindfulness is about cultivating a balanced view of the self, so that you can be open to receiving a balanced view of the people you interact with.

There are many great books on mindfulness and mindset, and one of my favorites is by Dr. Wayne Dyer. His book, *Change Your Thoughts, Change Your Life,* reflects on the eighty-one verses of the Tao written by Lao-Tzu.[11] He writes:

> *Rather than having judgemental thoughts about those whom you regard as separate or different, view others as an extension of yourself. This will diminish self-importance and allow you to let go of ego dominated thoughts.*

The Green Attitude knows that no matter what, "I'm not better than you, and you're not better than me," which helps us to avoid the hierarchies that perpetuate judgemental attitudes. There is an understanding that what lives in others also has the potential to live in me and vice versa. The difference is that I choose what will live in me, and I cannot judge the behavior, thoughts or feelings of others when I know that we are all here as equals. Otherwise, we're in a state of comparison.

Getting Out of Our Heads & Into Our Bodies

"I am a human being, not a human doing. Don't equate your self-worth with how well you do things in life. You aren't what you do. If you are what you do, then when you don't... you aren't."

WAYNE DYER

The ego doesn't like to be bored. Boredom for the ego feels like death. Boredom is confusion with the present moment. The ego is always looking for something to prove its existence. It needs to be *doing* something, instead of *being* content with the present moment. We notice the ego in children when they tell us in the most uncomfortable way "I'm bored!" I have come to learn that boredom is a gateway to creativity. When my daughter would tell me she was bored I would reply "great, I can't wait to hear what will become of this boredom you have". I could have fed her ego by relieving her boredom but instead I held space for it. From there I would witness her resistance and her discomfort and maybe a little tantrum to get attention. When we accept the comfort of boredom, it's like we're saying, "I see you" to the ego, which then weakens their presence. From there we tune into what it is that we need which opens up space for us to discover things that were once hidden, allowing for something new to enter. By becoming a curious observer of your present state , and your ego you give yourself permission to engage in an activity that is born from the present moment.

Perhaps you're thinking how you wish you could be bored because you're always too busy and have no time to slow down to be bored. That in itself is an invitation to enter into the practice of mindfulness. The truth is that there is no need to be *doing* anything. It's the ego that likes to *do*. While you're true self is content to just *be*.

So how do we get out of our judging and doing heads and into our bodies? With our breath. Right now take a conscious breath and you may notice your belly rise, or your chest expand. Breathing brings you into the present moment, because you can't breath in the past or in the future. The ego definitely doesn't like to stop in the present moment to breathe. Because the ego prefers to always be on the go and doing something. Breathing tames the fight or flight responses that the ego has so heavily been relying upon. I can go without sight, without hands and feet, without sound, but without breath, I'm dead.

I'm sure you've heard the saying "Don't just stand there do something!" Well when we practice mindfulness to get out of our *doing* and into our *being* instead we say "Don't do something just stand there" And what that means is, stand there in the present moment without judgment and notice your breath.

Developing Your Mindfulness Muscle

As you've been reading this chapter on mindfulness, you may have discovered that it's something you've never considered. The key to developing a mindfulness practice is found within its own cultivation. First, the concept is planted like a seed that starts growing in your awareness. From there, just like any seed that has been planted, it needs to be watered and attended to with sunlight and care. It's not something that you stand over and watch 24/7, but it does require a level of consciousness. Otherwise the seed will dry up, leaving you unfulfilled with an empty bed of soil

You can grow your mindfulness in a few ways listed below:

1. Mindful Walking: While walking slowly, take note of where you are and what surrounds you. Focus on each movement your body makes to take each step. Tune into the sound of your foot, and the sound of your breath. Feel

a sense of gratitude for your body as it allows you to move in the direction you want it to go.

2. Body Scan: Either upon waking or before sleep, starting from the top of your head, slowly scan through each part of your body until you reach your feet. As you scan through, notice any tension and mindfully soften that area with your mind. You can also tense, tighten, and squeeze your whole body, or just certain parts to bring awareness to it--and then release.

3. Guided Meditations: There are many of these to be found online to explore for yourself, depending on what feelings you wish to show more compassion towards, or grow more awareness of, be it anxiety, grief, sadness, or self-worth.

4. Formal Meditation: Sit with the intention to pay attention in a chair or on the floor. Hold your hands in your lap or place them on your legs. Do this for just one minute to start--every second counts! Work up to five minutes, then ten, then fifteen, up to twenty mins, or even an hour. Sit with the acceptance that you are going to allow any thoughts that come up without judgment while the focus of your attention is the sound and sensation of your breath. As thoughts enter, thank them for sharing, and then recenter by returning your focus of attention on your breath. You can categorize your thoughts when they arise such as, "This is a thought about work." Or, "These are thoughts about my relationship." And, "Okay, more thoughts about work," etc. Let them go, then return to the breath. Notice any judgements, and continually give compassion to the judging mind.

5. Mindfulness in Daily Activities: Set an intention to do the laundry from present moment awareness. Notice all of the steps you take from sorting the laundry,

noticing the colors and textures, and the smells and scents. Take it all in with a sense of gratitude toward the process. You can apply this to cooking, driving, cleaning, gardening, washing your car, etc.

6. After you've engaged in your mindfulness practice, the goal is then to take that focused attention of being in the present moment, into your everyday life. We'll never be 100% capable of being in the present moment for every waking moment, but we can always catch ourselves when we're not. Just the practice of *noticing* is enough to bring you back, even if just for a moment.

"Even not practicing is practicing in a way, if you are aware of how you feel compared with when you do practice regularly and how it affects your ability to handle stress and pain."

JON KABAT-ZINN, FOUNDER OF MBSR, MINDFULNESS-BASED STRESS REDUCTION

11

Purpose, Potential and Intuition

"Your subconscious mind does not argue with you. It accepts what your conscious mind decrees. If you say, "I can't afford it," your subconscious mind works to make it true."

DR. JOSEPH MURPHY, AUTHOR OF
THE POWER OF YOUR SUBCONSCIOUS MIND

Knowing Your Potential

I started writing this chapter with the title, "Potential: How to Reach It," but the word "how" stopped me in my tracks. This is because potential has nothing to do with the "how, " rather it's more about having an inner *knowing*. Some of us know exactly what we are capable of, while many others find themselves questioning their capabilities all the time.

Many times we say, "I haven't reached my fullest potential," and in that statement, we have the element of knowing. You know that you have capabilities for something more, so you go on to question *how*. When you ask how, you are a *human doing*, instead of trusting that you are already embodying your potential in this moment. Trust is the *human being*, whereas desire based on lack is the *human doing*.

Once potential is realized, the ego is no longer in charge. The ego doesn't like change--it prefers things to stay stuck and stagnant in suffering, or ignorant to what your potential is. This may have caused some discouragement or dis-ease for the ego, because it understands that there is a lot of work to do. It might feel too hard, or question their ability to make changes.

Let's turn to the Vedic philosophy that says that the goal of life is to awaken one's inner awareness or consciousness. Therefore, to come to know your potential is to go through the process of self-awareness, and making friends with your ego. I read the ancient Hindu scripture, *The Bhagavad Gita*, over ten years ago, and refer back to it often. This book helped me to see myself with the highest possible self-worth, as well as how to share a loving spirit with everyone else. The general idea is that: believing that we are limited causes suffering.

If someone sees something that they want, they might say, "I don't have that, and I want it so that I will feel happier." The Vedic view is that not only do you already have it, but it is a part of who you are. So your potential is already being met within you in each and every moment. Your purpose and potential are always noticed in the present moment. It's when we think of the future that we lose our sense of purpose and potential. When we are not aware of this we feel separation, and this separation brings on a longing, which then leads to suffering.

If I believe that my accomplishments are based on what I can do for others, then all I'm doing is supporting the potential in others––but not in myself. We must take care with the type of egoism that tells us that *doing* something will result in some type of reward from or for others. The Green Attitude gives without the expectation of receiving anything in return. This is how the Green Thinker will recognize in each and every moment what their potential is and their corresponding purpose.

A Red Thinker who is trying to reach their potential does it at the cost of others along the way. They may think they are winning as they leave a trail of victims behind them, but as we know, this is loss after loss. The Red's potential is based on what they can get others to see in them, or what they can convince others to believe about them.

I believe that our potential is found within our self-worth. If I don't feel worthy, then I cannot see much in terms of my potential. As my self-worth grows, so does my potential. This becomes a tricky area to navigate if my self-worth is based on *external* validation, because my potential will then be based on external recognition.

"Am I worthy enough? Is what I'm doing enough? Am I enough?" These questions circle to the question, "Am I living up to my potential?" To reference *The Bhagavad Gita*[12] again, Arjuna, a warrior, asks how to recognize a person who is self-realized. Krisha, a Hindu deity, clarifies that, "This state does not manifest in a particular physical manner, since it is a spiritual state." He says, "The self-realized person is one who is self-satisfied, regardless of outer circumstance, they are okay with it, good or bad." He continues, "They have realized grounded, experiential spiritual wisdom." In this way they are a person who is "free from all attachment" and "neither rejoices over good news, nor is troubled by bad events. They live in an established state of self-realization."

The day I realized my potential, was the day I realized my self-worth. I felt a sensation of gratitude and knowing in my body that what I was doing right now, was preparing me for what was to come next, even though I had no idea what that would be. I knew there was something more, and when that something more came––I'd be ready for it. It wouldn't be a shock or a surprise, it would be something I would openly welcome as a transition into the next phase of my life. Potential is not just what you will achieve in the future, it's what you can achieve in *the now*. In this regard, it's a living, breathing thing that is ever changing.

You might question your physical potential to do something or particular health problems that hold you back from reaching your potential. What you'll find, however, from researchers on energy and its connection to our physical and mental state, is that the way to change our bodies is to change our thoughts.

In Dr. Joe Dispenza's book, *Becoming Supernatural: How Common People Are Doing the Uncommon*[13], he says that it is a scientific fact that we use about 1.5% of our DNA, and if you think of your genes as a library of potentials, there are infinite combinations of gene variations that can be expressed. They're just waiting for you to activate them. Dispenza says, "It's all equal to your imagination and creativity." Our thinking is directly related to how we create our reality, which is essentially the expression of our potential. The more we catch insecure thoughts and bring them back to a Green way of thinking, the more we recondition and reprogram ourselves to a new mind and new being of unlimited potential.

What we think, we will become. We attract things into our life that we don't want when we focus on the things we don't want, because that's where our attention is. Alternately, we have the power to bring the things we *do* want into our lives by speaking about them, visualizing them, and *embodying* the feelings felt *while* speaking and visualizing about them. Your potential then, has no choice *but* to manifest into your reality.

Love yourself where you are now, and steer clear of

thoughts that begin with, "I'll be happy when...," or, "Things will be better when..." The truth is that you're already living in your potential each and every moment, especially if you allow your thoughts and emotions to exist in a constant state of self-love, non-judgment, and pure beingness.

Knowing Your Purpose

"With a purpose everything in life seems to fall into place."

JACK CANFIELD

You need to understand your purpose in order to realize your potential. Purpose is something that you already have, and your potential is what is still left to be seen. Reaching your potential is not something that you do, therefore there's no *how* to realizing your purpose either, because it's very much a process of *knowing*. I often think about whether or not there is a universal, collective purpose--something that we are all here to do. Or do we just have our own purpose? Is there more than one purpose? Can you choose your purpose? I'll turn to Jack Canfield for this one. He's the author of *Chicken Soup for the Soul*, and one of his most helpful books for me on this topic has been, *The Success Principles: How To Get From Where You Are to Where You Want to Be.*[14]

When you know what your purpose is, then you can act with clear intention toward that goal, and then everything else will fall into alignment with your life purpose.

Canfield says to consider these two questions:

1. What do you love to do?

2. What comes easily to you?

Next make a list of all of the times you felt the most joyful and alive in your life, then note the common elements of those experiences. Also feel free to ask others what they think you're good at! Whatever it is that brings you the most joy, is what brings you purpose.

When I was growing up, I knew from a young age that I wanted to *help people feel safe*. Everything that I chose to do after this had to align with this goal. So while in high school, I volunteered at the hospital in the late afternoons, delivering news flyers. When I was studying at the university level, I volunteered for the Foot Patrol, which was basically campus security. I'd walk around at night on campus to ensure student safety. I then worked as a bouncer in a popular night club, and then in a youth open custody facility until I finally settled into my job as a probation officer.

To ensure your success, it is crucial to engage in deliberate action aligned with your purpose. By consciously acknowledging the actions that support your purpose, you cultivate a heightened sense of this purpose, ultimately guaranteeing your path toward success. We need to invest time into our passions, because they are where purpose is born. The more time you invest in your purpose, the stronger that purpose becomes.

The Green Attitude can either be fully aware of pursuing their purpose, or they can accept that they are *in the process* of discovering their purpose. In this they will never doubt their purpose. Meanwhile, the Red Attitude will think of their purpose from one of two ways, 1) From the ego, which blames outside cues if they cannot pursue or understand their purpose, or 2) From a place of pursuing a purpose that is monetarily-based and for their own self-interest, instead of in the best interest of all.. This might look like a boss whose purpose is to become a millionaire. They don't care about their employee's well being, they just want their goals and salary to be met, regardless of the cost to others. They would celebrate reaching their goals like some kind of hero and give themselves all of the credit. Although you have the potential to become a millionaire, if you make this your life purpose, then you've already missed the point.

Our lives are most likely to have favorable outcomes when

we focus on our life purpose from a spiritual lens instead of a material lens. As a life coach, I set goals around my purpose to help others by aiming to enroll as many people as possible into my coaching program. When someone decides to work with me, my purpose is being met because I am helping them to learn how to love themselves and how to adjust their mindset to get more of what they want from life and less of what they don't want. A monetary reward is secondary. I know I have the potential to write a book with a purpose to teach as many people as possible how to change their thinking so they can change their life. Again, how much I end up making from the books I sell isn't the point.

This doesn't mean that I give things away for free though. As you recall me saying in the last chapter, the day I realized my potential was the day I realized my self-worth. I know the value that my coaching provides others and so I will charge accordingly. Of course I have to support myself as well and make a living like everyone else, so I do not undervalue my skills and expertise. Someone with a Blue Attitude may think their purpose is to serve others and ensure that everyone else is pleased and content, even if it means they have to make sacrifices to their own needs. If they were a coach, they may undervalue themselves and charge less than they're worth, or give away the books they've written for free. As we've seen though, this will come at a cost to themselves and will leave them questioning this as their purpose.

It can be said that when your purpose is realized, you start to experience a sense of freedom and empowerment. This is because living your life's purpose can be seen as an enlightening experience. Below is an exercise I give to all of the clients I coach, to encourage them to consider what their purpose might be. It's also from Jack Canfield's book15[15] I mentioned earlier, and it asks these three questions:

1. What are two of your unique qualities (something that maybe you hear people telling you all the time)?

2. List one or two ways you enjoy expressing those qualities,

especially while interacting with others.

3. Assuming the world is "perfect" right now, what would it look like?

Next you'll put it all together in a statement that sounds something like the examples listed below:

- "My life purpose is to use my compassion to support, inspire, and motivate other people's passions. My purpose is to help others freely express their thoughts openly and accept other perspectives with respect."
- "My life purpose is to use my humor and creativity in relationships, singing, dancing, and making music. By embracing our own unique talents, I'd like to build communities and tribes to share fulfillment with others."
- "My life purpose is to use my intuition, dedication, and meticulousness to solve problems and look at the bigger picture. I also wish to express these qualities with other people who are dedicated to their own personal qualities, with the ultimate goals leading to a happy, healthy Earth and society."
- "My life purpose is to inspire and motivate people by writing and organizing community events where everyone can freely express themselves from a place of happiness, joy, and peace."
- "My life purpose is to use my creativity and wisdom to connect with others in order to create a more peaceful, healthy, and joyous world."
- "My life purpose is to have fun and live kindly by sharing my humor and acts of compassion. Through this I hope to live with and around others in peace, acceptance, and support for each other without pain."

What you just read above are responses from clients in my program who have completed this exercise. Some of them remark afterward that their life purpose is just to be themselves, but who is that? Who are you? The trick to embodying this, is as simple as the saying below:

> Before enlightenment, chop wood and carry water.
> After enlightenment, chop wood and carry water.

This saying is derived from Zen Buddhism and highlights the idea that despite achieving enlightenment, or purpose, or potential, one's daily tasks and responsibilities in life remain unchanged. This means that you also remain unchanged. You're still you, regardless of your potential or purpose. Questioning who you are is what the ego does. You are still *you* regardless of knowing your purpose or not.

Trusting Your Intuition

While we are inching our way towards understanding our potential, which feeds our purpose, we need guidance from something deeper and wiser than ourselves. This is the voice of our inner knowing, our gut feelings, our intuition: a higher guidance system. We may have found ourselves pursuing a career that isn't in alignment with our core values and thus, isn't bringing us joy at all. We say this can't be what I'm here for. This can't be my purpose. And with that I say, sometimes we need to experience what we don't want so we can discover what we do want. We may have found ourselves on a path to destruction out of a place of fear, instead of a path to purpose and potential from a place of intuitive trust and guidance.

One of the most common questions I am asked is, "How can I know the difference between my intuition and a trauma response?" Trauma creates fear, while intuition is led by trust. If we are jostled by something that scares us and as a result we make a hasty decision that turns out to not be in our best interest, it's likely that we reacted from a trauma response. If we get a sense that something didn't seem right and we cautiously hold back in making a decision, then we are guided by intuition. Intuition is calm, guiding, and peaceful. A trauma response feels urgent, scary, and ungrounded. The intention of our intuitive guidance is to lead us to safety, not into fear.

We've all been there. Maybe you've just been laid off and you're scared that you'll go broke so you accept the first job offer even if it's not aligned with your values or purpose. Meanwhile you ignore your intuition that tells you that your dream job is around the corner and to turn this job down. Ten years later you're realizing how this all unfolded and need to find a new job. Many of the things we end up regretting are the things we decided to do based on a scarcity mindset, which only keeps us stuck and keeps us away from our purpose and potential.

You may say that you've never experienced your intuition speaking to you and in my experience working with clients who cannot access their higher guidance systems, I find that it's typically due to an inability to work in the realm of feelings and emotions. This is especially true for people who've been taught to ignore and invalidate their feelings, therefore ignoring and invalidating their intuition. Instead they keep feeding the wounded ego. If you've never learned how to have compassion for your feelings and emotions, they appear as unwanted guests, and telling them to go away results in the nullification of intuition. What also results is a lack of trust, and a lack of faith in yourself as you assume the *human doing* default programming.

Trusting your intuition feels strange at first because you feel like you're being irresponsible. The truth is that it's irresponsible not to. When we feel like something is off, this is our intuition telling us that we've gone off our path. But instead of following our own path, we keep getting back on the same road that everyone else is on. We think this is the responsible thing to do. We think this will get us there faster if we follow the masses and just do what everyone else is doing. We accept the discomfort that it doesn't feel right, and tell ourselves to 'suck it up' and 'just do the right thing."

When we find ourselves off the path and living a life full of resistance, we fall out of Green Thinking, and instead allow the intrusion of Blue, Red, or Purple thoughts in instead.

When we're off our path, we may feel overwhelmed, anxious, depressed, or health problems may pop up. All of these are messengers telling us we haven't been honoring the path of our purpose. The idea is to follow the path of least resistance.

Before I left my job with the government, I was doing everything that was deemed acceptable and mainstream by society for many years: going to school to get a degree, securing a good job, buying a house, getting married, having a child, and trying to be the perfect mom and wife. The more I grew intuitively, the more none of that stuff mattered anymore. This realization made me question if I was going crazy. Was I losing my mind? For a time, there were great fears about, "what will people think?"

I realized that trusting your intuition means not being concerned with what others think. I'd known for many years that I didn't want to be like everyone else. I knew I didn't want to be in a marriage anymore. I didn't care about owning a home or having a job with a pension and benefits. I didn't want to have to try so hard anymore to be like the other moms, I just wanted to be me! This is ultimately what inspired naming my coaching business: Free To Be You Coaching!

My intuition came as a gentle, guiding, loving push that said, "It's okay for you to do this, I got you! It's going to turn out okay." By spending more and more time in the Green Attitude, my energy was changing, opening me up to an entirely new world!

Thank you for sharing this journey of the *Colors of The Mind* with me. I hope that you learned helpful information and that you feel empowered to make healthy changes. Remember that you have the power within you to self-actualize and live in the Green mindset. You just need to tap into your inner voice and your deepest values, through conscious awareness of your thinking and emotional processes. You can do it, I believe in you. I saw these changes happen with myself, and now through my coaching business, I get to witness it happen to so many others. It is truly a beautiful transformation. Thank you for letting me share it with you.

Summary and Exercises

You did it! You made it to the end of this book, and I want you to know that just because you finished this book doesn't mean that you've finished your work on mindfulness, mindset, understanding your behaviors and taking responsibility for your feelings. It simply means that you have more information about yourself.

Now it's time to Take Action!

To help you with this next step involves getting out there in the world and speaking to other people about what you've learned. That is an important part of learning is being able to "teach" but even more important is to be the change that you want to see in others. You need to be a role model and show others how your authentic being is emerging.

The Behaviour Sequence Tool

Here you will see the terms used earlier in the chapter regarding Outside Cues, Inside Cues and in the last column are the rewards (cookies) and punishments (boots). This is one of the most confronting exercises to do as it shows you the thoughts behind your behavior as well as what needs your behavior fulfilled (inside cookies). You'll typically choose a behavior that you regret or that left you feeling confused, and I'm sure you'll be giving yourself a bunch of 'inside boots' for this because we're always the first to find fault with ourselves. But finding the inside cookie (the good things) about your behavior may be trickier. For example: Specific Behavior - Yelling at my daughter, I might not think there's anything good about that. But the cookie I get from that behavior is a sense of being able to express my anger. Meanwhile I end up getting outside boots from my daughter for speaking her her in this way, and then I give myself boots as well.

The key lies in looking at the Inside Cues for clues as to how I could have responded to her in a different way, with a different way of thinking. The most important step is to go into the thoughts you listed in the Inside Cues and attach a color attitude to each of them. From there you can go on to see how you can make those thoughts more Green and effectively see what different behavior would stem from those thoughts instead. Remember, *neurons that wire together, fire together*, so what you're doing is creating new neurological pathways.

(2)	(4)	(1) Start Here	(3)
OUTSIDE CUES People/ Places/ Things	**INSIDE CUES** Thoughts/ Feelings/ Memories	**Specific BEHAVIOUR**	**OUTCOME** **Inside Cookies** **Outside Cookies** **Outside Boots** **Inside Boots**

Decisional balance exercise:

You can use this tool when you are unsure of the path to take. It will give you a visual of what the "good" vs the "not so good" things are about certain circumstances or habits you have. I've used this tool with clients who struggle to know whether to stay in a relationship or even to sell their house, or quit their job. Some use this tool if they need further insight to lead them in the right direction regarding their substance use or other addictive behaviors. After filling it out the "visual" outcome will be obvious as to what it is you need to do. I also encourage you to go back to the "Good things" about staying the same in the first square to see how you can get these needs met in a healthier way.

Good things about continuing with this behavior	Not so good things about continuing with this behavior
Not so good things about changing this behavior	**Good things about changing this behavior**

Use this acronym to help you decide whether or not a though is useful it's called THINK

True
Helpful
Inspiring
Necessary
Kind

1. Ask yourself, "Is this thought true?" Remember not all of our beliefs are true, although they seem very true to us at the time.
2. Ask yourself if your thought is helpful, chances are it's not helping you at all and instead it causing you anxiety
3. When you find out if the thought inspires you or not that can be a big "ah hah" moment. It's like some of the people we keep around in our lives that do not inspire us, so too with our thoughts, why keep them around if they don't really have anything positive to offer us.
4. From there, asking if the thought is necessary is an interesting one because sometimes it is necessary to have the thought just so you can have the opportunity to challenge it.
5. Finally, is the thought kind to yourself and others? We can be very unkind to ourselves in the way we think, and equally in the way we think about other people, which brings us back to the question, is this thought necessary?

Notes and References

Preface

1. Officers in the STICS group demonstrated significantly higher quality scores on Structuring Skills, Relationship Building Skills, Cognitive Techniques, as well as the global Effective Correctional Skills. (Public Safety Canada)

STICS was developed by researchers at Public Safety Canada in the mid2000s to improve the effectiveness of community supervision STICS training was reserved for POs supervising medium and high risk clients. Attitudes represent a major risk factor for future criminal behavior and are considered to underlie other criminogenic needs, such as substance abuse and family/marital relationships (Bonta & Andrews, 2017). Officers were taught how to alter procriminal attitudes using cognitive and behavioral intervention techniques. This included, for example, teaching concrete prosocial skills through modeling techniques and cognitive restructuring Bonta, J., Rugge, T., Bourgon, G., & Wanamaker, K. (2019). A conceptual replication of the Strategic Training Initiative in Community Supervision (STICS). Journal of Experimental Criminology, 15(3), 397–419. https://doi.org/10.1007/s11292-019- 09371-4

Chapter 1

2. Esther and Jerry Hicks, The Law of Attraction, United States, Hay House, 2006, page 30

3. Napoleon Hill, Think and Grow Rich, New York, Random House, 1963, page 14

4. David R. Hawkins, The Map of Consciousness Explained, United States, Hay House, 2020, page 73

Chapter 3

5. Gabor Maté, MD & Daniel Maté, The Myth of Normal,Toronto, Alfred A. Knopf Canada, a division of Penguin Random House Canada Limited, 2022, page 24

Chapter 4

6. David R Hawkins, Letting Go, United States, Hay House, 2012

7. Sadguru, Karma, United States, Harmony Books, 2021, page 105-106

Chapter 8

8. David R Hawkins, Letting Go, United States, Hay House, 2012

9. Dr Paul O, You Can't Make Me Angry, Torrance, CA, Capizon Publishing, page 45

Chapter 10

10. Stephen Mitchell, Tao Te Ching: A New English Version, New York, HarperCollins Publishers, 2006, Verse 49

11. Wayne Dyer,Change your Thoughts-Change Your Life, United States, Hay House, 2007, page 50

Chapter 11

12. Commentary by Swami Sadashiva Tirtha, Bhagavad Gita for Modern Times, New York, Sat Yuga Press, 2007

13. Dr Joe Dispenza, Becoming Supernatural: How Common People are Doing the Uncommon Page 139, United States, Hay House Inc. 2017

14. Jack Canfield, The Success Principles: How to Get from Where You are to Where you Want to Be. New York, Harper Collins, 2005, 2015, page 26-27

15. Jack Canfield, The Success Principles: How to Get from Where You are to Where you Want to Be. New York, Harper Collins, 2005, 2015, page 26-27

Printed in Great Britain
by Amazon

47393955R00099